WILD HONEY

Also available in this series:

Wild Honey

ALISON UTTLEY

Illustrated by
C. F. Tunnicliffe

LARGE PRINT

Oxford, England
Santa Barbara, California

British Library Cataloguing in Publication Data
Uttley, Alison *1884-1976*
Wild honey.
1. England. Social life, history, 1837-1914
I. Title
942.081092

ISBN 1-85089-524-4

Printed and bound by Hartnolls Ltd, Bodmin,
Cornwall
Cover designed by CGS Studios, Cheltenham

ACKNOWLEDGEMENT

Grateful acknowledgement is made to Ruth Pitter for permission to use on pages vi and 83 two brief passages of poetry from her book *Urania*, published by The Cresset Press.

There in the bank of the brook, the immortal secret,
In the ground under your feet the treasure of nations,
Under the weary foot of the fool, the wild honey.

RUTH PITTER

CONTENTS

CHAPTER ONE

The Ladder to Writing

Style is the manner of writing, the fashion and beauty of the expression, the way in which the art of writing is performed, and style cannot be learned by rules. Nobody can become an artist in words unless the art lies within his mind. One cannot take lessons in style, but writing can be improved by taking pains in the presentation of the subject. The artistic quality which is called style is a gift of the gods, a birthright which will come into being without extraneous help, although that help may quicken the seed and bring forth the flower earlier.

The seed may wither if the art is never put into practice, or it may stay alive as a power of appreciation, a critical faculty with no practical expression. Style cannot be taught, but it can be influenced and assisted in its birth. When it comes into being it is a personal attribute of the writer's, unique as his own character.

As a gardener tends his soil so the writer can help his seed to fruition. Most people think they can write at least one book. It is the easiest thing in the world, they aver, to take up a pencil and scribble a work of art. "My life would make a good book," they say, but they do not produce the book, they say they have no time. It remains unwritten because they have not the knowledge of their own tongue. There is more to the writing of a book than the mere possession of a vague plot.

Where can the art be learned? Painters go to the Slade, musicians study under various masters and then go to an academy of music, but writers have no such help. They may take the English school at a university, but this is not a training for writing books. It is not an apprenticeship in the art of writing.

Fundamentally writing demands a knowledge of syntax of the language, rules which are taught at school, with parsing and parts of speech, all very dull but necessary for everyone, whether a writer, blacksmith or housewife. Children are taught to write essays, and this is at best a small help to the would-be writer, and often a hindrance to originality of thought.

All my ideas of being a writer were shattered by the essays and their structure as I was taught in my youth. Our essays were a test of good handwriting and an absence of blots. I could attain the former by exerting the greatest care over forming each individual letter, with loops unfilled with ink, but smudges and blots always were a hazard.

We had to provide our own paper for essays and this was a problem, for money was scarce and paper was even more rare. My parents drove me to the little town a few miles away and we inspected paper in the high-class stationer and bookshop. I chose "Sermon paper", on the advice of the lady who owned the shop; it was an expensive packet of shiny thick paper of loose leaves and ivory surface. It was fit for a bishop at least and I felt very proud to possess it, with a new "Waverley" pen and a new bottle of ink. Our bottles of ink were always watered down to make them last and a thick sediment lay at the bottom, to be brought up on the tip of the nib by the unwary writer.

They come as a boon and a blessing to men,
The Pickwick, the Owl and the Waverley pen.

The advertisement for my pen was everywhere, on railway stations, and in newspapers. It must be right.

I felt inspired by my sermon paper, and I wrote with extreme care, underlining the title and the headings with red ink. I wrote my essays on the bare scrubbed table, white as a bone, in the kitchen, with the cloth, the plates and cups pushed back to make room. Men walked through the kitchen, carrying cans brimming with sweet frothy milk, doors were wide open to the wild winds which blew across, and the lamp flared up, or candles blew out in the draughts. Tales of horses, cattle, revival meetings, circuses and robberies went on regardless of my presence, and I gazed dreamily at the kind homely faces around me as I struggled to find words to describe a Shakespearian character, when the live characters out of the past were already there. Phoebe and William, Audrey and Touchstone were playing their parts, and Bottom the Weaver was whittling the sticks, and I had only an inkling of the truth of time itself, time past and time present mingled there.

Then somebody going through the kitchen from the back door where the troughs lay, to the side door, with a large square basket, squeezing between my Windsor chair and the oak dresser, nudged my arm violently, and a long streak of ink fell on the white page. That was the direst calamity and it often happened to me. Ink was the arch enemy. I had no indiarubber, for I was careless over such trifles, they got lost or borrowed, and a crust of bread was always used at home. Even a sharp penknife came into use to scratch out a blot, although it occasionally made a hole to rouse the anger of my teacher.

So I went on with my essay, but my words never came to life. I could not use my own experiences, the pithy talk of the countrymen I knew, the tales I heard, the awareness of earth, and woods and fields, which were the kernel of the life around me. There was no spark of inspiration, I was cut off by the inky smudge which took possession. It was the symbol of my life, a struggle between the perfection of a sheet of white paper and the rugged proximity of people, but I could not bear to sit by myself in another room in solitary grandeur, away from the great fire and the hissing copper kettle, from the ticking talking clock and the tales of the travellers home from the fields. I might miss something vital by my absence, some old story of long ago, some exciting incident of the present, with fox's cunning or the humanity of an animal. So unconsciously I laid a store of memories, warm and life-giving and the sterile essay languished for want of food.

Nobody could write even a humble essay without some idea of the subject, and my attempts were dull with no gleam of light or fancy because I was afraid to wander from the beaten track of conformity. Individuality was not encouraged. No essays were set on country subjects, and we were all country children. Essays were read aloud by the teacher who would pounce on anything that gave a chance for sarcasm. The girl who compared the moon to an incandescent light, in the evening sky, was mocked at before the whole class.

It was the most exciting light anyone had ever seen, this modern incandescent, but afterwards we kept the moon in her place, with no imagery. The moon was our friend, our companion and guide, more personal than a relation, and we did not wish to bring her into disrepute.

Once, in an essay upon "The Novel", I found myself involved in near disaster. I had never read a novel, and indeed the word "novel" meant something loose and immoral in my strict home. Dickens was read aloud, and so were George Eliot's *The Mill on the Floss*, and *Adam Bede*, but these were homely household books about country people. Novels were something different, wicked.

There was a novelist with the romantic name of Marie Corelli, I had heard her name when some visitor spoke to my mother about her book *The Sorrows of Satan*. She had the authentic aura of the novelist, who was acquainted with the Devil himself. Such a book was not for us, although I dearly wanted to know what were the sorrows of the great king of Evil.

I wrote my essay with imaginative flights of fancy about novels, as I discussed various categories of books which might exist in the great world of literature. No children were more ignorant about novels than we, with no libraries and no books, and parents who read the Bible. I divided novels into books of family life, such as I knew, dramatic novels such as *Treasure Island*,

and *It's Never too late to Mend*, for we read the
"novels" of Charles Reade, Dumas, Stevenson,
with delight. *Sherlock Holmes* and *The Moonstone*
came into this section of novels. Finally I
ventured on novels of passion, where passion
had the old meaning of the word, hot-tempered
clashes, and wild feuds. Scott was in this list,
but unluckily I gave the names of two authors
whose names I had heard, but whose books I
had not even seen, so I did not know their titles.
Thomas Hardy and Grant Allen, and I added
Marie Corelli with some misgiving.

I gave in my essay neatly written on the
sermon paper, and I had a feeling of satisfaction,
for it was longer than usual, and there was
something in it. Never a smudge or blot defaced
the pages, and my heart rejoiced. To my
surprise the town headmaster, who had set the
essay in a spirit of enquiry into the lives of his
unknown country pupils, came white-faced and
bitter-tongued to the class. He waved the bundle
of essays, he scolded everybody for their rubbish,
but I got the worst of his flow of anger, which
poured in a spate of wrath, scalding us all.

What did I know of novels of passion, he
demanded? What could a schoolgirl know of
passion? What had I read of Hardy, or Grant
Allen, or Marie Corelli?

"Nothing sir," I murmured truthfully.

"What did you mean by passion?"

I was too frightened to reply. He was in such

a passion himself that I was intimidated and scared out of my wits. I thought of the hymn, which we often sang with my mother.

When bitter words are on our tongues
And tears of passion in our eyes.

I was a passionate child who should curb her hasty words, I was often told, but I did not discuss this with the master. I was mocked at and scorned and degraded by the man's tongue. In adult life one never has the humiliations and agonies of childhood, nor do we feel the pricks so acutely. I never wrote an essay at school with any ease after this, I said as little as possible, and only in exterior examinations could I do well.

School days were no preparation for the art of writing, except in one respect. Latin was a compulsory subject for Matriculation, which we had to take. It was the ancient language of the earth, the tongue of trees, and we read legends I never forgot. Somebody gave me a copy of *Smith's Smaller Classical Dictionary*, and the stories of the gods and heroes become my daily reading, with the Bible for company. The dryads lived in our trees, I had always known the water nymphs in our river and in the springs, the fauns in the woods and Pan himself in the pastures. The world was peopled by the figures of mythology, and I accepted them as true.

Poetry, already a part of home life, came again with the Odes of Horace, which we read with an imaginative teacher. Cicero, Virgil, Ovid, we read slowly and painfully, with many a struggle, but the task of translation, the search for words, the grammar, all gave an appreciation of words and a realization of choice offered to us. This teacher also advised us to read books by Thomas Hardy, in spite of the ban by the headmaster, and I found the life depicted in the books very similar to tales told by my father of his childhood, in our farmhouse, with shepherds and ploughmen, guisers and fairs.

The Bible was an everyday book, and I listened to the stories in the beautiful terse prose from my earliest years. It was not archaic language, for many of the words and turns of speech were in use among us. People used the second person singular, and they often used poetic phrases culled from their Bible reading. Every night before we went to bed we had the prayer, "Lighten our darkness we beseech thee, and by Thy great mercy defend us from all the perils and dangers of this night".

"Perils and dangers", that closely aligned pair both enchanted me and made me shiver with apprehension, for the doors were barricaded, shutters fastened, the big keys turned in well-oiled locks, the huge wooden bolts were drawn across, an iron bar was placed across the front door, falling into a socket. Ever since the house was built and the ancient house which had stood there before it, the doors were barred, and these measures were taken against perils and dangers that lurked outside. Everywhere is a frontier, and the outposts must be on guard. Robbers and highwaymen once, goblins and witches now, haunted my nights, although I was not sure they even existed, but the prayers kept them at bay.

The stories I heard read aloud from the Bible gave me a sense of literature such as I had from no other source. The seed lay dormant in my mind, for I had no desire to write, I was afraid of mockery, I was unsure of the art which required pen and paper. I made up stories and never wrote a word except in little home-made books of stitched sheets of notepaper, cut small. I received a silver medal for English, but it was for work on Shakespeare and poetry, not for any talent in writing.

Later, when more books came my way I fell under the spell of Joseph Conrad. He was the first writer whose prose fascinated me. I was alone in my admiration, nobody else read his books. I had fallen in love with something else by that time, I did not care a button for any essays, and writing had the rival of mathematics. I was taught by a master who took the place of the fierce denouncer of essays, one who showed me a language I could understand, more exciting than English or Latin, a speech of signs and patterns, a musical language, and this new view of mathematics came when figures were left and symbols were used, the Greek letters, the sign of infinity, the signs for the differential calculus. This salved me, it was a power, and we felt we were gods at play. Long explanations and statements could be expressed in a few letters and symbols, we saw this symbolism as a key to immortal knowledge.

I sat on my bedroom floor each night with a candle by my side and queer shadows fluttering over the ceiling, as I worked at Conic Sections, going from one example to the next, transforming them into reality. The ellipse was one of the beauties of this early work, a curve which enthralled me as far away and long ago someone must have discovered the circle. The bridge, the cantilever, the parabola, all were like music. We wished to turn everything into shapes and symbols, for the course of the earth itself and the stars were mathematical shapes.

So I went off at a tangent to study physics and mathematics, and English became the lost and forgotten love. Sometimes there was a tug at my heart when I came across a poem, a book of fine prose. A physics lecturer lent me *Diana of the Crossways* to see if I could bear it. I was lost in the story and the wonderful way of writing of George Meredith, and I borrowed every book of Meredith's and his poetry to satisfy my craving for it. This tutor spoke to me of the link between Philosophy and Physics, and made me aware of the writing of some of the ancient physicists, so that I read their lives.

Then came Turgenev, from a woman tutor, and the clear limpidity of the style was like spring water, and I read every one of the row of pale yellow books. If ever I wrote I would choose to write like Turgenev, I decided, with no knowledge of the difficulty of attaining such simplicity. After my Physics Honours degree I would study English, I thought, but I went on to Cambridge with a small scholarship to study education, psychology and philosophy. Here essays had to be written each week, the first since schooldays. The subjects were interesting — Rousseau's Emile, on Country schools, on Pestalozzi's life, — on children's imaginations. There was a good reference library, too. The essays were not scorned and there was no heavy sarcasm. One's grammatical faults were corrected, and we were encouraged and praised. For the first time I received positive help in writing, and I enjoyed writing in my little room overlooking Fenner's. For the first time I was drawn to literature, but I was still bound by strong ties to science. I was told these two loves were

antagonistic, but I did not believe this. Science and literature could go hand in hand, each showing one side of life. I visited the Cavendish laboratory where a friend was a research student, working on cloud formation. This was worth all the writing, I felt, to be in at the exploration of the sky.

I wanted to write a book but I was not ready. The words would not settle themselves in any pattern, I had not found my style. It was too soon. I knew I wanted to write of the country as I saw it with all its beauty and serenity, from within.

Once I sat with pencil and paper in a bedroom at my old home, determined to write the feelings that flooded my mind before I went away. I could not do it. I was too near the subject of my desire. I stared at the beech trees on the horizon, like a cock's comb straggled against the sky. I could see the water trough, the shapes of stones, the flowers, the ragged man who sometimes walked there picking up sticks, the old pack road.

Not until I went away from home and brought before my inner eye the vision of the pack road and the shaggy wood could I capture it in writing. I discovered that remembrance is the sieve through which the experiences must pass to remove the extraneous matter. To write is to paint a picture, not to take a photograph. The plot is unimportant, but the presentation of the plot is the unique possession of the author. Time passed, years sped by, I wrote nothing, but I scribbled impressions — sunlight on a field, the wind beating the trees and the swaying of the branches, pleasures I wished to keep. One day I went up to the attic of my Cheshire home, a room that had been the playroom. It was very quiet, all sounds were dulled up there, and I looked around with pleasure. In a gable, like a doll's house in the large attic, was a tiny pointed window and below it stood an old Pembroke table from my child-days, banished there. It looked enticing, this small intimate little room within a room. I fetched pen and paper, and sat down to write. I drew around me a cloak of silence, and within its shelter I worked. I told of my country home, for I was filled with longing to write of that place before I forgot the spell that bound me to it.

As I wrote I became a child again, living in the kitchen, peeping in the parlour, walking in the woods and avoiding the stones, alarmed, secretive, alert, frightened, happy, and alive as I had never been since those young days. I felt each sensation as once I had experienced it. I opened drawers and cupboards and saw things I had forgotten. They lay there waiting, as if they were in an unseen world, out of our time, existing in eternity. I could even smell the strong odours of the house, stuffy, mildewed, scented, according to the room, and I heard voices as if I were there. It was a miracle, and I felt sick with the intensity of the vision, as I scribbled my thoughts. I was caught up in the web of time remembered, just as Proust returned to his childhood drawn there by the taste of a brioche in a cup of tea. Hours passed like minutes as I secretly wrote. It was not memory but a return in time, and I was exhausted when at last I went downstairs.

I finished the book, I cut it shorter, I copied it out on a borrowed typewriter which I could hardly use, and I kept it secret for the old fear of mockery was strong. I was justified, for unwillingly I was prevailed to show the copy and even the beginning was scorned as "not the way to write a book". It was too simple, too childish even to read.

I threw it in a drawer and forgot about it for some months, and then I read it again and sent it to a publisher, but it was returned with a word of praise. I tried again and it was accepted by my present publisher. It was something living, it was an entity with a life of its own, and I felt the joy of a creator.

The subject-matter of a book is not of immense importance. I wanted to write about my home because I loved the fields and woods so passionately, the birds, the flowers, the little grassy paths which nobody could see unless they were pointed out, the invisible ways of rabbit and sheep, and a human child. I wanted to paint in words the effect of the clouds and the sun over wide spaces of land, when everything is united, part of the world, and in harmony with it.

The tale must leave in the reader's mind a perfume, a modicum of pleasure, a quality of the feeling that was in the writer's mind as he wrote. This feeling, this essence pervades the reader's remembrance when the subject of the book is forgotten. It lingers on, a fragment of remembered happiness, a glimpse into some place not on earth. It is a haunting of the mind by beauty, by immensity of space, by the immortals as if they had appeared for a moment and shown their luminous faces. I had seen them and I knew they were there. Perhaps this gets through to the reader but probably circumstances, the time and place are against the revelation, but when it pervades the reader's mind there is an affinity between writer and reader, and the reader has a moment of bliss in making contact with the unknown.

So the writer weaves a spell to capture the heart of the reader, and it is an individual enchantment, a "supernatural windfall", accepted with humility if it occurs, lost if it is denied.

Memory is a weak and shallow possession, and few people can remember a book completely when they have read it, but various episodes, the feeling of a white road, the scent of a herb patch, remain, to bring the story to mind. Something is recaptured, and it is this that the book exudes, the smell of country days, of the sea, of a fetid town, a pleasure in the simplicity of the tale which has no ornamentation, no richness, except its own private worth.

CHAPTER
TWO

Some Pleasures in Reading

Most of my early life was spent in reading, for pure pleasure, and, like a drug addict I concealed my intense longing for books by various devices of secrecy. There was a time for reading, and a time for helping others, and my father often asked me in exasperation "Can't you find something better to do than reading from morning to night? If I read all day who would feed the cattle, or plough the field, who would milk the cows and fettle the mare? We should all starve and so would all the live stock." I did not answer, I put away my book and waited and then I took it out again and went on with the tale. One of the reasons for just anger at my reading was that I became deaf and dumb. I did not hear when anyone spoke to me, I was lost in another land and in another time than ours. I still have this power of concentration in a book, so I dare not read in a train lest I get carried past my destination. In writing a story I am completely absorbed, forgetting time and place and people.

Poetry has always been my favourite reading, and it coloured my life before I knew even the alphabet, for my mother sang or recited poetry every day, and the lilt of it filled my early years. Ballads of Robin Hood, old country ballads, pious stories in verse, hymns for the young, all led me on to seek rhyme, but there was a dearth of the printed verse except Longfellow and Tennyson, which I chose for my birthdays. The sound of the verse, the swing of the rhythm meant more than the sense, and the music of poetry was always ringing in my mind. A young man, whom I thought to be very old (he was in his twenties), gave me a copy of Browning from his bookshop, and so introduced me to a poet who was a favourite for years. A girl at school brought a Shelley to lend me, and I read avidly, taking it all to myself for my own. Later on Walter de la Mare's "The Listener" came with the impact of a vision of the future, a revelation, and I sought for more of his poetry, to read in fields and lanes.

The books were read out of doors, for there was peace in the country with no motor cars, no sound except the singing of birds and the bleating of lambs. Even these rural sounds faded away as I drifted into another world, sitting under the oak tree, or at the end of the garden by the herb patch. The literary memories are mixed with the scenes where I read the books, or heard the tales read aloud to me. *Adam Bede, Romola, The Mill on the Floss*, were kitchen books, warm and contented, with the great copper kettle singing softly on the hob and the grandfather clock ticking gently with its changing note, as if the clock was aware of what it heard. Dickens too was a kitchen book, and it brings the smells of baking, of brewing, of horses, of milk cans and farmyard to me, as I absorbed these odours with my reading. The nightmare which often followed some of the horrors of Dickens came afterwards when I went upstairs with a candle shielded from the draughts, held against the shadows which threatened me with knives and robbers and shrieking females. *Wuthering Heights* nearly drove me to the madhouse, I was so frightened by the story which seemed deeply akin to all I knew. I imagined a hand on the window, clutching, knocking, tapping, and the tap of the rose tree was enough to make me quake and shiver. I read this book in a grim little north country inn where I had to stay with my husband who was doing some engineering work in the bleak hills. Snow fell all day, the place was dirty and gloomy, and I found this book at a small twopenny lending library in the village. It possessed me in an uncanny way, terrifying me, as the gales roared down from the moorland,

and the ugly village with its steep street and the bare little inn were part of the Yorkshire setting for the tale. *Jane Eyre* also gave me this vivid horror as the madwoman (the first of my acquaintance) shrieked and I sat alone, listening to her voice, waiting for the knife to strike me.

Pastures, stone walls, wooden gates were the safe familiar backgrounds to my reading, and they brought comfort of touch in times of fear. A rug spread on the lawn for *Paradise Lost*, and the wild winds of Shelley and the school book of *As You Like It*, made a friendly feeling and an intimacy with Heaven and Hell. George Macdonald's books were very real to me, events happening in our house and land, the horse in the stable, the goblins in the lead mines. I frightened my brother and myself by relating the tales of the goblins tapping, as unconsciously I tapped and we listened.

I never read in a wood, although the great woods surrounding my home were as familiar as the rooms of the house. There were dark rocks, lichen-bossed, uprising in massive stature from the sea of bracken, with seats roughly carved by nature in their shapes, but I did not read there. The woods possessed me with their own spirit, and who knows what I might have seen, what spirit of primitive man, what faun of mythology might have risen to confront me? Even in the fields, as I read in the silence with my back to a tree, so quiet that the silence deepened till I was unconscious of this world, I was sometimes aware of a deeper stillness than anything on earth, and I tore myself unwillingly from my book to look up and meet a pair of amber eyes regarding me, a weasel standing near, a fox, a bird, and I felt I had nearly been captured and taken away to a world not my own. This feeling of the proximity of another world than ours always pervaded me. I might be seized by a

tree's long branches and held captive; I might enter a rock and have to stay there for a thousand years; I was invisible and aware of other invisible shapes around me, claiming me, for my defences were down when I read and I was vulnerable.

In youth a book was a treasure of diamond and pearl. It was something bound in gold, a secret revealed to the listener, a private possession for myself alone. We had no idea of the number of books in the world, of the making of books, and each was unique and beyond price. Historical novels gave me great pleasure, so Scott was welcomed, in spite of the small type, and the poor paper on which the tales were printed. The books cost a shilling in the village, they were bound in red cloth and I re-covered them in brown paper. Witches and warlocks, knights and fair ladies, filled the pages and filled my mind as I read *Guy Mannering, Kenilworth, Ivanhoe, The Talisman* and *Peveril of the Peak, Rob Roy* and others. I was utterly enchanted with Scott's novels which displaced Dickens from my thoughts but not from my inner consciousness which was always haunted by some of the characters. *Kim* and the "Jungle books" followed, bringing a new world, India, and strange magic.

Then came Thomas Hardy, in a clandestine way, for *Tess* shocked my mother. I lived in a Thomas Hardy country, and our ways were his ways. The love tales were those of the village people. The fields and barns, the singing of the waits, the churches, the shepherds with their smocks, were all known to us. Even the sale of a man's wife was an incident in my father's youth where there had been a similar happening. I read every book of Hardy's and also the poetry. Then I found Henry James, and again I read each and every book, with Meredith's complete novels. I liked the style of James, the involved sentences, the classical women, the plots. Joseph Conrad came before James, from a book a friend had bought on a railway journey. It was called *Youth*, and I read it under the fir trees on the edge of the lawn, with the fields and hills around me. I felt my own youth, my ignorance, my insularity as I read of the great seas with their storms and their ships. This was my first book of the sea and of seafaring and foreign travel, and I read every book Conrad wrote. I read as I walked along the white roads where only an occasional horse and cart went by, I walked with the book held in my two hands, with my eyes fixed upon the printed page. I heard the roar of the sea and the river sang by my side, as I went on that limestone road, under the trees, among foxgloves and dog daisies and meadowsweet pools, to the station, to the post-office, to carry out various errands for my mother. So the sound of the river, the scent of flowers was mingled with the smell of foreign lands, the dark-skinned natives, the traders, and the lovely heroine, the great beautiful ship herself.

The only ship I had known was the one from which Robinson Crusoe had been wrecked. We had no seafaring people among our ancestors, we were country bred and the sea was a mystery. So Conrad opened my mind to receive impressions which never faded, and no sea books ever had the same intensity for me. Robert Louis Stevenson, admired and loved, had not this power, although in *Treasure Island* he came close to it. Long John Silver tapped with his stick down the paved path to our door, and he came in one night and lured me off to sea, but he lacked the effect of Joseph Conrad, that master mariner, whose descriptions of waves and vast spaces were never excelled.

The great Russian writers came to me from some unremembered source in my late teens. I do not recollect meeting anyone with this introduction to Dostoievsky, and Tolstoy, to *The Brothers Karamazov*, to *Anna Karenina*, to *War and Peace*, to Maxim Gorki whom I read at night in the dining-room at our farmhouse, with shutters barred and a great fire burning, and a candle lighting the room, making long shadows on the thick curtains. "Time to go to bed. It's past ten o'clock," said somebody coming in with another candle but my lesson books were spread on the table, mathematics and physics, and nobody knew I was not reading these. In extenuation I confess I got as much excitement and allure over the mathematics adventures and the new ideas of the structure of matter as I did over the Russian writers.

After these Russians came Turgenev, whose yellow books were on the shelf of a College tutor. I borrowed them, two or three at a time, and read them all with joy and appreciation. The country life portrayed was akin to our own country's feelings, I could understand and enter into the lives of these Russian aristocrats and peasants, and I was the peasant, although I felt like the aristocrat.

I read *Flatland*, a book on two-dimensional world, lent to me by a tutor who was a wrangler, with whom I talked about other dimensions of space. I read the lives of famous scientists, Faraday, Newton, Sylvanus Thompson, Tindall, and I adored Oliver Lodge and Rutherford and Sir J. J. Thomson. These books too were read in fields and lanes, among foxgloves and buttercups, with the sun streaming down and the Irish haymakers walking past me with their forks and rakes and wicker-covered beer bottles. I knew I ought to be helping them, and sometimes I took up a rake and worked at the long green furrows, turning the grass to dry in the sun, or tedding it with a fork as I repeated to myself some formula I wished to remember. The modern novels of that period were never read by me because they were unknown. Somerset Maugham, the Bensons, Hichens, were popular novelists I never knew, but Anthony Hope's *Rupert of Hentzau* came from a girl at school, and *The Scarlet Pimpernel* caused a flutter in the dovecot of my mind.

I have never been a great reader of novels, and I met Miss Austen's novels only when I was grown-up, when they were read aloud to me to lure me by their magic. I realized their wit and their subtle mastery of the English language, but the characters were outside my experience, and my desires. They lived in a world of great houses, of many servants, of balls, and I felt like little Fanny, in *Mansfield Park*, an adopted poor relation spying out the land.

I read books over and over again, I enjoy turning back to passages which have been my delight once before, with the added luxury of knowing what is coming. I am like the little girl in Ernest Dimnet's story, who sat in the Paris train reading a dull dry book, completely absorbed and lost in its contents. Dimnet suddenly asked the child. "What are you reading so delightedly?" The girl looked up, called from some far away regions. "Monsieur, c'est *l'Histoire Romaine*, et je vais arriver à Jules César." "How do you know you are coming to Julius Caesar?" he asked. "Oh, I have read this book many times," she replied.

So one can return, lost to the world, to enter a time and place and to stay there, tasting the joys, refreshed by them, savouring the magic and delight of the meeting with old friends.

CHAPTER
THREE

Country Craftsmen

I was brought up among craftsmen, certainly not among machine-men or even bookmen, and I was used to seeing things made by hand, either up in the Master's Chamber (my father's workroom), or in the barn, or down in the village at the wheelwright, the blacksmith, the carpenter's shop.

Willa Cather speaks of "that irregular and intimate quality of things made entirely by the human hand", and this quality came into being with all the things we had. When we wanted hencoops we made them at home. There was the planing and sawing and hammering, and out from the workshop came a clean, neatly made hencoop which the hen entered as if it were a beautiful little house.

When we wanted a wall mended, the stone-waller came to do it, and my father helped him. It was a work of great skill. I stood near watching them lift the great stones and fit them in the dry walls, with a chip here and there by a stone hammer to make them the correct shapes. The servant boy also stood near to give a hand and to learn the art. Wall-making was an important piece of craftsmanship, for walls were made to last a hundred years. The large stones were fitted neatly, on a strong, broad base, and the coping stones along the top were cut to a rounded shape. Flat stones made layers in the walls, and these stones added to the strength of the wall. In places of importance a stone with a flat surface projected a little to make a half-hidden step for climbing. We knew where these secret steps were but they were almost invisible to strangers. We kept these private stairs as meeting places, and parcels or even letters might be placed there hidden on the grass.

My father's hands were beautiful, I always admired them although I knew nothing about hands. They were the clever hands of a craftsman, who could mould and carve and finger very small objects as well as large ones. There was nothing clumsy about them and he could take up the most delicate object of flower, feather or ornament and see its beauty. He was ready to invent a device for foiling a fox, for keeping a horse from opening gates, for growing a choice flower without glass, for bringing spring-water to a new place by methods of irrigation in the rocks. He made roads on the land.

The spinning-wheel had worked in the corner of the room, and he often spoke of my grandmother spinning there. Beer was made in the brew house, a little stone room, and we looked at the density stick which was inscribed with measures and used to make the beer of the correct weight. Candles were made at home in his boyhood, and medicines of every kind from herbs in the garden and fields, from goose grease and various animal fats.

When we wanted a summer-house my father built one of stone on the edge of the lawn, a little square house with a door and a window. He roofed it with timber, rising to a pointed pinnacle at the central apex. Round the wall inside he put a wooden seat and there we played at Robinson Crusoe or I kept my dolls. He helped to build one of the great barns. All countrymen knew the working of stone in that county of stone, just as they all knew how to thatch a stack and make an ornamental tassel at the end.

Fences were made in the stackyard, chairs and wooden hay-rakes were mended in the Master's Chamber, but gates and ladders came from the village. It was grand to see the rakes fashioned and the wooden teeth put in. Saucepans, kettles, milkcans and churns were soldered on the steps near the kitchen, and it was one of the joys to watch the long silver stick of solder and the soldering iron red-hot from the kitchen fire as the silver drop filled up the hole. I had the pleasure of seeing this same work in France when a travelling tinker sat at the gates of an ancient town in Southern Provence with an array around him of all the old kettles and pans in the town which he was mending with skill, to the music of a flute and tabor which called the people to bring their utensils. The trade of the tinker is one of the most ancient, and the tinker is not a gipsy, but a real craftsman with inherited facility.

A travelling tinker called occasionally, to mend the tin, brass and copper vessels in general use, too badly damaged for my father's mending. He was heralded by barking dogs, and calling children, and an air of excitement. He set out his small furnace and heated his soldering iron, sitting on the steps with the broken metal around him. We stood near, watching with fascinated eyes to see the silvery solder (called sodder), as it filled the holes under the tinker's skilful brown hands. He was dark as a gipsy, with raven hair and quick speech, with magic in his fingers, a descendant of tinkers who have roamed this country since the Middle Ages. He tapped to hear the ring of bell-metal, he whistled and muttered, and he sang a snatch of wild song, as he went on with his work. He could make a small toy out of the scraps of metal melted in his crucible, and he bought up any bits we did not want.

We hunted in the chambers for worn-out saucepans, a century old, hidden away there. Our own tin saucepans were tall as top hats, made to fit the stove, to hang over the flames of a dying fire. They were very old and he mended them with care, recognizing their good metal and their character. Copper and brass, he looked at them all, the little pans to poach an egg, the large ones for preserving fruit and boiling puddings. Whole hams were boiled in a large iron "kettle" with a lid and a flat handle. It took two men to lift it. The Irishmen also had a great kettle of their own for cooking, and it was kept in the barn. The tea-kettles, a brood of them, were copper, blackened with age and smoke, and all had to be kept in order by the tinker.

"Tinker, tailor, soldier, sailor,
Rich man, poor man, beggar-man, thief."

we chanted as we counted our plum-stones, and of these the tinker, the tailor, and the beggar-man were our familiars. I always hoped I should not be obliged to marry the tinker.

In former times most countrymen were craftsmen, and they did their repairs because they knew how to do them. When we wanted a low wall which had to be decorative as well as useful, my grandfather and his brothers built such a wall about two feet high and eighteen inches wide. They fetched stone from the woods, splitting off the lamina in thin sheets, and trimming the blocks, and fitting them over the low wall to form a comfortable seating wall which has lasted a hundred and fifty years. Nature took a hand in it, and planted stone crops and ferns in the crannies. Cowslips seeded under the south side, and bird's-eye spread a carpet of blue on the bank. We used to have tea on this wall, and everybody rested there as a convenient place to look at the view.

When we wanted hinges or bolts we went to the blacksmith and he made the nails too. When we wanted harness the saddler made it. He repaired the saddles, he stuffed the horse-collars, he stitched reins, and a new pair of reins was something to be very proud about.

The wheelwright made a new cart, and it was painted in bright colours, according to our desire. We went to the wheelwright's yard to see this done, and to watch the men make the great wheels in the pit. The love of colour is strong in country people and I admire the carts I see in the Buckinghamshire villages. A four-wheeled wagon, majestic as a ship, which we saw in a field near Boarstall Castle in the gated road, was painted canary yellow picked out with blue and I stared enchanted at the beauty. We kept away from these canary and lemon yellows, but we had deep blue, almost ultramarine carts and scarlet ones were often used.

The painter used decorative designs, little

scrolls of snow-white panels of contrasting colour. The spring cart, which was made by a coach builder, had lovely lines on every spoke of the wheel and every facet of the high side. I remember standing with my parents to gaze in deep content and admiration at the spring cart which had just come back from the coachmaker where it had been re-sprung and re-painted. We gazed at the dark, green cart with its white lines, which glittered and sparkled when a wheel was

spun round on the jack. Milk carts were yellow, pony traps were navy blue, gigs were golden yellow, manure carts were scarlet, farm carts were bright blue and red, and wagons were also blue and red. The constructional lines were picked out in white, as if to show what a fine thing it was.

The farm carts in Buckinghamshire have not always these gay colours, but colours are present in the houses, whereas our farms were grey stone. Here the old rose-tinted red brick, with the timbers natural or painted black, make colour enough in a village. In this county of Buckinghamshire, where wood takes the place of stone, I have been deeply interested in the crafts I have seen. Men working with their pole-lathes in the woods are craftsmen in a limited sense as were the men working with lathes in the hill villages, cutting and polishing stone ornaments.

Buckinghamshire, a county of woodland, has a great tradition of furniture making. A few years ago one could see the bodgers at work in the woods making chair legs on a simple pole-lathe which had a living tree as part of its structure, in the woods at Great Hampden and Speen. Some of them may still be there, doing their craftsman work, and there are small household factories which make complete chairs. I used to visit a famous craftsman, Harold Goodchild, the chairmaker, in his cottage at Naphill. He could make a beautiful Windsor chair from start to finish, beginning with the tree which he cut down, to the final result. He bent the wood for the curving bows in a manner of his own devising, and he carved the splats for the chair back, using old traditional patterns which he varied by his own artistic splats. It was a joy to watch him in the little shed packed full of parts of chairs, close to his cottage. In the orchard wood for seasoning was stacked, and from it he chose his pieces, yew or elm, beech or ash according to the part of the chair. For these chairs have various woods in their structure, and often a chair is made of at least three kinds of timber. Mr. Goodchild died a few years ago and his individual work is still carried on by those who worked with him and shared his integrity in good work. There is an enthusiasm for a chair made by one man, as opposed to a chair assembled by many people, and more love goes to the making. I always wish my childhood villages had included chairmaking in their crafts, but stone was the source of the work, whereas in Buckinghamshire the crafts depend on the beech trees.

Although factory methods are used, good country work is sent out more speedily, and most of the carving is done by hand. Many of these wood-carvers use their talents in making articles privately and one can see charming toys or carved chests, or small pieces of furniture made by these men in their spare time in the evenings. There is a strong feeling for working in wood in Buckinghamshire, and beautiful carving is inherent in the south.

In the Buckinghamshire churches we think of those craftsmen of long ago who had art in their fingers. The master mason carved the portraits on the capitals of the pillars giving them a freshness and a living sense, a cynical smile or a knowing wink, as if the men who made them were getting their own back against the church dignitaries. The faces are human, probably portraits of worthies who were caught and turned to stone. When a church is renovated, probably a modern inhabitant of the village is enthroned there among the sculptures.

Artists painted the walls with frescoes and decorations such as we see at Little Missenden and Little Kimble. There are figures of St. Christopher and St. George and St. Francis, and Our Lady weighing souls against the Devil, and Salome dancing with her beautiful curved body in its transparent veils, swaying back. The wood-carver made the misericords and poppy heads, with great freedom, finding the face in the wood, suiting the design to the material. I think of the carvings at Edlesborough and at Stewkley, and at Maids Morton. The worker in iron, the blacksmith, made the iron bands on the painted chests and the handles and hinges of the great doors, and the nails with square heads and a cross upon each. Gold and silver work have disappeared and probably it was not made by the village craftsmen, but the smith made the wrought-iron stand for the hour-glass at Edlesborough Church to hold the glass which timed the long sermon and he made the beautiful little weathercock of the centaur at High Wycombe Guild Hall.

A number of cottages are thatched and one can see a thatcher at work any day of the week in the Bucks villages. There is the long ladder and the thatcher combing the straw on the roof, with a great pile of straw lying on the ground below. The thatcher works to the right of the ladder and the tools are thrust in the straw to his left all ready for use. A long bind of withy holds down the thatch, and a thatching needle is used. We had our own thatcher, belonging to a family of thatching ancestry, and he put the neat roofs on the stacks of hay.

In the village of my youth, a few miles from my home, there were self-supporting trades and crafts upon which the economy of the place depended. It was a misty-blue village, of stone-built cottages, with a squire and a parson, and a long winding hilly road and market square. Hills encircled it and fields were adjacent, behind the cottages. It was very workaday, sleepy to the casual eye but full of hard-working people, who were craftsmen and proud of their work.

Wheelwright, carpenter, joiner, stone-mason, and cooper, tinsmith and blacksmith and boot-maker, all had their "shops", and their regular jobs, and all we knew and visited on Saturday morning. There was a noise of hammering and sawing, of tinkering, of shop bells and horse bells, of wheels and muffled sounds which commanded us to stop and stare at the goings-on. There was time to stare, and I looked with vivid interest, for it was the great wide world to me.

There was the brewer, who lived in a Queen Anne house, with horse-mounting-block, and lace curtains and maids, opposite his romantic brewery in the old thick-walled mill. He made beer and stout which connoisseurs praised, for he used the local water which sprang out of the earth in a clear fountain and ran through a tiny aqueduct to an ancient mossy water mill, whose great wheel entranced me as I gazed at it, dripping with water. The sweet smell of hops pervaded the scene. We called here each year for a barrel of beer for the Irishmen at harvest time, chosen with care and ordered some months earlier for maturity. The Irish were very particular over their drinks. Men brought the cask from the brewery and settled it firmly in the cart, when there had to be an adjustment to balance it. Accessories to the brewer's craft were made in the village. The casks were made by the cooper, the spigots and wooden taps and the wooden funnels (which we called by the old name of tun-dish as dishes used in a tun or cask) fitted into the bung-holes of the casks. Wooden butter-prints and Scotch hands, wooden milk-pails and small wooden churns for butter, and dollies for washing day were turned in the village.

Clothes pegs were made by the wandering gipsies, who always sold a good length of these delightful little doll-like pegs when they came to our door. The gipsies were craftsmen who made baskets, rough but unique in their way, and very cheap. They had rustic baskets put together from small branches, mossed and picturesque, and these they lined with moss and filled with ferns from the woods.

Wooden milking stools of traditional pattern were made in the country town, and stools of many kinds were used as alternatives for chairs. A servant sat on a stool and so did a child. Three-legged stools with scarlet or blue seats were the presents for children, who sat on the hearth, close to the fire. These were made in the villages and sold for a shilling. Wooden skewers, and pins for doors also were made, and much used. Iron hooks which hung from the ceilings and beams of kitchen, larder and dairy to keep goods out of the way, and to dry them, were made by the busy blacksmith. He also fashioned the long pokers and the tongs and shovels, but the tinsmith made the bright "hastener" and the trivets and Dutch ovens which hung before the fires.

A friend and neighbour is a real modern craftsman, for he can make anything, carve a detail, and above all he is a mender of the trifles that are loved. He puts a new wooden leg on an old Dutch doll whose straight, painted leg disappeared half a century ago. He pegs the new leg into place so that it swings to and fro in the nonchalant manner of an active Dutch doll. He mends a brooch which the puppy has bitten to a shapeless mass, and he mends a grandfather clock which occasionally defies the laws of time by striking a hundred without pause, instead of the midnight hour. He can put a ship in a bottle, and make a musical box play its tunes. Like Doctor Cornelius in the ballet *Coppélia*, he brings life to the inanimate. He delights in repairing children's toys and he brings new vigour to the worn-out toys of the nursery.

All is done in his spare time, for the love of the craftsmanship, and he pits his wits against some mechanical detail, which he overcomes. He reminds me of countrymen who used to make toys for their children out of slips of wood carved with a penknife by the kitchen fire on winter nights.

His hobby is to bring life to the crooked and maimed in the world of the inanimate. He says he would like to spend his days of retirement when they come, in travelling round the world with a small workshop on wheels, to restore the broken toys of childhood for all nations. Some men are born craftsmen, and whatever their path in life those who have the magical touch exercise it in well-doing for the pure pleasure of creation.

CHAPTER
FOUR

Possessions

People might be divided into two categories: those who like possessions and those who are content to own nothing. The former are despised for their desires, which are associated with greed and materialism, and all the evils of this world. The latter are revered and admired as the saints who are beyond earthly pleasures, who build up treasure in heaven and care nothing for the good things of this life.

Saint Jerome is painted with a book and a writing desk, a crust of bread to eat and a stream for drink. The rocks are his shelter, the cave a sleeping place and he has the lion and perhaps an owl for company.

I look with envy at this scene of simplicity; it is like childhood, when I went to the high woods, and lived each wonderful day in a rocky enclosure, with a silver birch growing in my house, a stream for water trickling near, forget-me-nots carpeting the floor and rocks for table, and chair. Wood pigeons and blackbirds and wrens were my companions and my reading was a fairytale book. Except for slight anxieties about weasels and badgers and foxes I was free as air with no desires except to live there all my life.

The stable with the manger and a heap of straw was enough for the Nativity. The holy ones had no possessions, for they possessed all things, and the world of the visible and the invisible was theirs. I could make my home in our stable, with a lantern hanging on the wall, and the half-door open to the moonlight, the black mare standing in her stall and I with a three-legged stool and a book, safe from interruption. The mare was my friend, but she was not my possession and although I loved animals with intensity, feeling that only they understood my wants and my jubilations, they were not my possessions for they were never possessed, they had free-roaming souls unbound by man. For in childhood I was not a possessor, liking my own things, fiercely protecting them from other eyes; but sticks and stones and trifles were invested with magical powers, they preserved me from evil, they made a ring of enchantment around me to keep me invisible with their ancient magic. It was the rocks themselves with their rough texture, which were possessions of value.

Now I belong to the possessors, I adore things, and I enjoy them so much no heaven would be complete without a few objects of my own, even a flower from earth, a shell from the sea, a feather from an angel's wing would content me, but it must be my very own, not to be taken away by any immortal. I could never be a Communist, I like possessions too much. I realize this as I get older and see the accumulation and know the beauty which is inherent in them all. For the possessions carry the sense of the divine, running through the objective world, the god-like beauty which is present in material things.

There are the pots and pans of everyday life, of the kitchen and table. A little brass saucepan, which makes delicious meals and sits firmly on the electric stove as if it had known it all its hundred years, is one of these things. There is a crooked little knife, bent and worn, which does all the work and puts to shame the fine knives with ivory handles. A wooden spoon joins the domestic company, for wooden spoons have great attractions. They go back to primitive times when the first man cut a spoon from a slip of wood with his sharp-edged flint and gave it to a woman for her soup. There is a feeling of history about a wooden spoon, and we remember the love-spoons carved by Welshmen for their ladies, and the wooden spoons used by our grandmothers in the vast kitchens. I have seen wooden spoons made in a small Buckinghamshire factory and I am glad they are still to be bought in spite of the coloured plastic usurpers, for nothing can take their place.

Forks are not so important, and one could go round the world with a spoon and knife, and never miss a fork. They were fripperies introduced from Italy in Elizabethan days, to be used by the rich. Plates I cannot resist for my list of possessions, a green Wedgwood plate belonging to my grandmother, and used by me for dessert. A little pewter plate, a tiny Rockingham plate, a Platt plate with a view of Italy, which was the Sunday cake plate of childhood. Bowls are very important, old lustre bowls with deep blue and a pattern of flowers, a brown stoneware soup bowl, a Chinese bowl and a Chelsea bowl, and of course a wooden bowl, for wood and stone are the two most desirable substances, better than gold and silver. I have no stone bowl, I left mine behind at the farm of my childhood, too heavy for me. It was a quern, which had been used by some ancients for grinding corn, and I used it to grind wheat ears and barley by thumping in this aged utensil, but the Robinson Crusoe flour I made was too gritty to eat, and the quern was neglected and left in the garden. A pair of eighteenth-century lustre candlesticks of glass are possessions, for their beauty and for the pendant crystals which catch the sun and the fire and send rainbows into a room. A small blue Wedgwood cup and saucer from my grand-mother's days is good to drink from, and even the saucer was used by old country people who found their tea too hot for comfort. A tiny teapot matches the cup, but it is very small. The lid is made of pewter, and this toy was kept in a high cupboard in my childhood for safety. It was called mine — and I inherited this trifle. Little teapots have a great charm, they are so absurd, they hold only a few spoonfuls of tea, but their shapes are entrancing. Perhaps they were made for children in the eighteenth century, and it is a miracle they have survived.

A doll's tea set in silver I must have, among my possessions. This tea set consists of a teapot, a coffeepot, a cream jug and a sugar basin, the size of acorns, and this would go in my pocket in times of peril and flight. It could be filled with nectar in another world than this.

The miniature has always attracted me, and my oak cupboard holds tiny vases made by country potters for small wild flowers, and tiny glass jugs and bowls for daisies. These are not in the high rank of possessions, they are the property of dolls. There are tiny books too, some volumes of Shakespeare and very small volumes of *The Iliad* and of the Greek New Testament, of 1831. A possession I must have is a very small chest of drawers, made of oak, dating from the early eighteenth century, with five little drawers. A small bureau of Queen Anne's time is another possession, useful and beautiful, with tiny brass handles and well-fitting inlaid drawers, and a look of perfection. They are replicas of larger pieces of furniture, traveller's samples, made for journeys by coach through England at a period when roads were unsafe and customers could see these miniatures and order the large furniture from them.

Books are collected, but books are a specialized section of possessions, too vast to be considered, ranging from an early copy of Hans Andersen to the Redouté roses and the Thorncliffe *Temple of Flora*, a library of books which cannot be carried about. One's copy of Shakespeare's sonnets, marked in the margin, annotated, loved, is something to take through life, as an epitome of all else.

To return to the things made of stone. I would put among the most treasured an egg made of Blue John, that translucent magical spar from our rocks, dug in the Derbyshire hills, polished delicately with a stone lathe and dripping water from a spring (for the spar splits and breaks easily). The Blue John egg I could carry through the fields of Paradise or the fires of Hell, to keep my fingers warm or cool, to give me courage or to share my content. An element of magic and earth-worship is present in this egg, or in any object carved from stone. I become a primitive, filled with adoration for stick and stone, revering this object out of the earth itself, made in the fires of earth's interior. The admiration for this possession goes back to my earliest years, when I first saw the stone in rough purple rock, like violets imprisoned in crystal. I heard of my mother, who at the age of six spent her scanty savings on a small nest of stone with four tiny eggs of Blue John, which she took to her mother, who was dying. The nest was given to me but the eggs had already disappeared. It was years before I was able to buy an egg for myself. It cost sixpence at a country bazaar, but now it is worth six pounds, according to the crazy modern values.

Money value does not come into possessions; it is something else, a link with the past, a glimpse of the future, a touch of felicity inherent in each object, but through all runs the strand of beauty. A series of planes exist in the Universe, and one is a slow-curving plane, hardly in time at all, where beauty exists in its own right, often intangible — a phrase, a turn of speech in *Romeo and Juliet*, a spark of light, a dream. It is the dream in the Blue John egg, in the tiny silver tea set, in the old bent knife, the wooden bowl and all the trivial objects, that makes them precious to me. Jewellery is the desire of many people with a craving for possessions. The inner sparkle of the diamond, the lustre of the pearl, the fashioning of gold, beaten and twisted in a fine shape, are sought and kept.

Once I inherited a diamond, which gave me great interest, but only as a source of income if I had to sell it. I could not get to terms with the stone itself, it was not in my world. One night I opened the door to look at the sky after a great storm. The moon was shining over the drenched world, and the rain fell gently, softly upon the garden. Then, in a bay tree by the door I saw a diamond, more beautiful than mine, glittering in the moonbeams, shining red as fire. I moved and it became a vivid green and this changed to blue as I turned again. The green was like that of a glow-worm, shining close to me. I bent low to look intently. It was the spectrum coming through the large raindrop, which hung on a leaf, an enchanting sight, and it humbled me, it was so pure and strong in its colour. A diamond indeed! I fetched my diamond and put it close to this rain diamond, and as the moon caught the gem it was difficult to distinguish between the two, but the raindrop was the brighter jewel. It gave me a new value for my diamond, a new vision. It was a raindrop frozen in stone, which I could see when there was no rain, and no moon. I carried a raindrop with me, captured from the earth. The world is full of diamonds I realized, if only we could see them. There is an invisible and inviolate world where these treasures exist free for all.

A blue moonstone in a slim circle of gold is another possession, given to me by my husband when he left for the front in the 1914 war. It was the moon itself, changing its colour and depth with my own anxiety. A crystal cut into the shape of a heart was my mother's gift to me when I was seven, a relic of her own childhood. It was a constant wonder to me, and I wore it on Sundays suspended round my neck by a black ribbon, my only jewel. I held it to the kitchen fire and saw a score of pointed flames dance in the facet of the cut quartz. It was magical, an entertainment and a revelation of the beauty of light. It was kept in a kitchen drawer with my blue velvet Easter egg, and is still a humble treasure, for it carries in the starry interior the hopes and fears, the anguishes and agonies of childhood, whose troubles were assuaged by a glimpse of the sky-blue Easter egg and the crystal heart. Nobody could be unhappy with such treasures.

There is a second category of possessions in the great realm of pictorial art, the possessions of mankind, the inheritance from the work of great masters. These pictures are owned by the onlookers who take from each painting a spiritual reality, and awareness of the content of the picture, a store of beauty which flows like water from a spring. They drink at this fountain, they stand in the shower which falls upon them, and they make it their own. These onlookers, the ordinary people, possess the pictures in a special way, and their possession is that of someone who listens to a Beethoven symphony, lost in the world of music, who watches the sky and sees the shooting star. So I return to the National Gallery, to seek out certain pictures which I regard as my own private belongings. I hasten to find the Rembrandt portraits, a Patiner landscape of silver tone, the Poussins, the Chardins, the little girl with an astrolabe, by Mabuse, the Breughel Nativity, the Carl Fabritius self-portrait, and I meet my friends whom I know so well. Vermeer, Botticelli, and Van Eyck are my immortal possessions, free from time and space, never desired, in reality, but always there for those who love them.

As one looks at these pictures, there is a suspension of time, the seconds are stilled, and the pendulum stops. A new and incredibly exciting world is opened, and one enters the door. Then, slowly, there is an awakening, one moves away, bewildered, refreshed and changed by the vision of eternity. The picture hangs there, to shed its benison on the next visitor, who may accept it or may refuse, but something can be taken away, a taste of its timeless beauty.

Some of my possessions are so ephemeral they last only a moment of solar time, but eternity in another layer. The light falling through the bare trunks of the trees early in the morning, at dawn when the rising sun shines in long fine rays of piercing intensity and these golden beams strike the trees with ardour, as they powder the trunks in gold. I try to catch this moment, when every mote in the air is touched by the sun. Once a child asked me where the Unicorn lived, and I showed her the light which appears between the trees, illuminating a land where anything might happen. Many possessions are nearly invisible, shared by some small creature perhaps. A spider's web with the dew on it, hanging in a rose-bush, a feather on the lawn, the burnished case of an insect, seen for a moment and known intimately, and then lost. Some are eternal — the moon, remote, changing, in the misty sky, Orion appearing in Autumn, a planet at evening, a cloud against a copper-blue sky. A cuckoo in April, a blackbird in May, all of these are possessions which we treasure and we hope they are enjoyed by the dead as well as by the living.

If thou didst ever hold me in thy heart
Absent thee from felicity a while
And in this hard world draw thy breath in pain
To tell my story.

CHAPTER
FIVE

Kitchen Gardens

Two hundred years ago Joseph Addison wrote: "We have always thought the kitchen garden a more pleasant sight than the great orangery, or artificial greenhouse." The kitchen garden still holds pride of place in gardens, although it has changed a good deal from those days of the eighteenth century. The wonderful kitchen gardens of fifty years ago are no longer with us, for they have departed with the great houses which they adorned. There are not enough gardeners, or enough houses to support them nowadays.

Still, when a large country house is opened to the public in the summer months, the people always linger in the trim little kitchen gardens behind old red brick walls, or by the stables and outhouses. The kitchen gardens are not on show, but strangers slip behind the screen of privacy and they marvel at the rows of vegetables, they longingly eye the ripe gooseberries on the sturdy bushes, they stare at the rich red strawberries, and admire the peaches. This is an earthly plot where all good things grow for the benefit of man.

I am drawn to a kitchen garden as if pulled by a magnet, and it is a nostalgic love for the place, for I have no kitchen garden of my own. The green rows of carrot tops with a glimpse of the orange red carrot peeping through the soil, the onions with their bent tops, the celery in its trench, all these in mathematical rows fascinate the looker-on. We are filled with admiration for the orderly, the neat, the straight lines of the regimented plants which flourish so happily. How unlike the sprawling plants in the herbaceous border, the unruly roses and the untidy phlox and asters! The vegetable garden is a child's toy of symmetry and design, which we wish to play with.

The kitchen garden which I remember had these same straight lines, and no footmark must be left on the brown soil. Peas and scarlet runners were trained up their sticks, and waved their tendrils at the top as we walked between with baskets or colanders to pick a green load. It was not a task but a pleasure, to be hidden in the arching green with the sun unable to penetrate, and the ripe pea pods hanging close to one's nose. The carrots were admired for their foliage and I picked the coloured fan of ferny leaves, which were often touched with red as if by autumn. The ferns were used in vases among the roses and sweet peas. Then there were the fat little lettuces, each with a good heart, succulent and firm, which we washed in the trough as we went back to the kitchen. Outside leaves were stripped away for the pigs and only the centre heart was kept. Little white turnips were also eaten boiled, and we nibbled scraps of them raw when they were peeled.

The kitchen garden was a larder of good things and we ate so much we had no appetite left for the dinners and suppers which awaited us. Everything tasted much better raw and fresh, and we sampled and nibbled and bit our way round the garden.

Our kitchen garden was in the shape of a triangle, two sides of which were bounded by a stone wall, and the third by a hedge in which many birds nested. In a corner was a heap of pea-sticks and robins always made a nest in the impenetrable jungle of long sticks. Paved paths went round the garden, and a path down the middle so that it was easy to be dryshod in wet weather. It was the old garden that had been there for generations and the soil was deep and rich with constant manuring and working. The apex of the triangle was the herb garden, cut off from the rest by the narrow stone path. A wooden seat against the wall stood in this part of the garden, shielded from sight by the bushes, and there, by the herb garden, among the bushes of rue and sage, of fennel and dill and camomile, I sat, serenely lost, as I played with dolls made of poppy heads and beads made of seeds and fruits, or I read a book.

Like all good old gardens this did not belong exclusively to the kitchen; it was also a flower garden in parts, and the flowers and fruits and herbs grew happily together with incursions from the fields. White violets grew in masses, never uprooted, and they spread among the

roots of horse-radish down the smaller side of the scalene triangle, which faced the north. The garden was on a gentle slope as was everything in our country where nothing was flat. The topside faced south and under the wall grew the important bushes, the red currant and black currant which kept our shelves filled with jam, for the berries were heavy with juice and grew in such quantities even the birds could not eat them all. Human children rivalled the birds among the currants, which we regarded as grapes, transparent and sweet, hanging in big clusters, but still there was enough for all.

In the centre of this side of the garden, where the path bisected the triangle into two equal parts, was a white rose tree of great age and fame. It had always been there, I was told, a rose of heredity, old-fashioned, sweet scented, with grey-green leaves and flowers of many petals whorled around a green boss. There was a hint of fawn colour, or the palest rose pink, in the rose's centre, and I think this aged rose must have been an Alba Gallica. We picked great bunches throughout the summer and took them to friends on every visit. It was a fountain of roses rising from the earth and spreading its fragrance over the garden.

Below the white rose, grew a bush of thyme, very large and outflowing in a myriad little spires of grey-green, a bush I visited every day for thyme was an important ingredient in cooking, and I was the "thyme-picker". Next to it flourished a spectacular root of red cowslips, which my father had propagated himself from a cowslip root. The flower heads were heavy with florets, the colour was rich and ruby red, and the scent that of a field of cowslips. There were no weeds, for somebody weeded with great thoroughness, and it was not the children of the house.

On the right of the white rose were the single

red Damask roses, with their golden stamens and whitish buds, flowers I was sent to pick for the house. With a cherry tree, they filled this border. The centre of the garden was devoted to the vegetables in their neat rows, drawn parallel to the base of the triangle, from south to north. They had always been planted in this way.

One or two apple trees grew by the centre path, easy to reach when the orchard was too wet to enter, but they were not important trees, unlike the enormous tree which was as large as an oak tree, near the gate in the base of the triangle. This great tree was very old, but it was still a huge cropper. Little green apples lay on the ground and they were collected for pigs, and we had them for our games of Robinson Crusoe. I learned to count with green apples which I picked up on the lawn. There was an owl's nest in a hole in the apple tree, and the whole tree was reputed to be hollow. It was so old nobody could remember when it was planted, but it dated to the days of my grandparents. Under this tree the cream cheeses were buried for ripening. It was a sacred tree to me, the one from which the Serpent gave Eve an apple. The garden gate was the gate of Paradise from which Adam and Eve were banished, and I saw them there, with the angel and his flaming sword of sunlight, as they moved away, heads bowed, weeping.

Adam and Eve in Paradise in the kitchen

garden, was the theme of my inventions and my thoughts, and I knew what they liked as they wandered there, tasting the good fruits of the earth.

Parsley bordered the centre paved pathway, in a thick green bed in which it was possible to conceal a doll. Gooseberry bushes grew along the bottom edge of the footpath, with the fruit hanging ripe and the birds all ready to eat it. Sometimes a wasps' papery nest hung in a gooseberry bush like a pale grey football, and the berries on that bush were red and gold, for nobody dared to pick them. Jays and magpies entered the garden, and pheasants boldly came to eat, defying the gun which was ready to shoot them for the table. The garden was populated with bird and animal life, and scarecrows stood among the beds. It was a warm happy corner, with its ferns and wild flowers, its roses and fruit, its vegetables and its surprises. The lilac tree by the garden gate seemed to welcome all to enter the garden and to taste the good things. The gate itself made a creaking sound and clicked its latch to warn those within to get on with their picking and to stop eating the fruit.

Other kitchen gardens in the neighbourhood were on the same pattern, with a stone wall and rows of vegetables neatly arranged, and here and there a rose tree or a root of blue primroses or hollyhocks. They were warm, for they were shielded by the wall from the north and open to the south.

Every visitor was taken round the garden to see the progress of roots and plants. One portion was given up to the early potatoes, but the main crop was grown outside the walls in the ploughfield. Outside the walls too, a short distance away, was the kitchen garden's companion, the orchard, and we stepped across the lawn and climbed down a flight of steps built into a high wall, to reach the orchard which was on a lower level of the hill.

It was only a little green orchard with no charm of roses, and the shade of the trees made it a much cooler place than the garden. It was surrounded by a wall except in one place where a hedge bounded it. A pony lived there all the summer, or a cade lamb, or a calf or two. The orchard had its own animals, which disturbed our games, when we went to climb the apple trees. It also had the clothes-line with the family wash every week.

The trees were tall, and they bore big crops of apples, when the ladders were taken down the steps through the tall gate into that domain. Clothes baskets lay at the foot of the trees and the servant boy climbed high to pick the apples while we ran underneath gathering the fallen fruit from the long grass. The varieties were Keswick, and Brambling, and some pippins, and yellow apples which melted in the mouth. I have these same yellow apples in my Buckinghamshire garden, with Russet apples, James Grieve.

On my bookshelf is a little Gardener's Calendar, dated 6th April 1842. The title is written in copperplate across the stiff paper cover. The original binding disappeared over a hundred years ago, the book must have been much used, and William Stiles who owned the book in 1842 rebound it in good, thick, cream paper stitched with thread.

It is an excellent little book, divided into the months with their work, lists of flowers and vegetables to be sown, and work in garden, in hotbeds and on lawns. The end of the book has some general advice which is helpful even now, and I mean to follow some of the instructions.

"To destroy slugs" is impracticable for most people, except those with live stock.

"When the slugs, caterpillars, etc., begin to appear, turn ducks into the garden, once or twice a week; but never keep them longer than two or three days at a time, as they will soon tire of their food or become indolent through satiety. While in the garden they should have no food given to them but a little water is necessary."

It would be a pleasure to welcome a duck to be indolent, but ducks are scarce in my neighbourhood. To "Prevent the Blossom of fruit trees from being damaged by early Spring frosts" is a valuable hint.

This appeals to me, for in recent years we

have had hard frosts when the trees are covered with blossom. I hang newspapers up in a ghostly manner, with poor results, for it is impossible to cover a tree with paper. "If a hempen rope be intermixed with the branches of a fruit-tree, in blossom, and the end of it brought down so as to terminate in a bucket of water, and, should a slight frost take place during the night, in that case the tree will not be affected by the frost; but a film of ice of considerable thickness, will be formed on the surface of the bucket in which the rope's end is immersed; 'although' says Dr. Anderson, who made this experiment, 'it may happen, that another bucket of water, placed beside it, may have no ice at all upon it.'"

This should be an interesting experiment, as I believe some gardeners hose their fruit trees when a frost is imminent.

Dr. Anderson's method of preserving apples from frost is another gardening tip.

The apples are kept in a small compartment, under the roof, where there is no fire, which is therefore the coldest part of the house. "Yet it is found by experience that if a thin linen cloth be thrown over the apples, before the frost commences the fruit under it is never injured. Linen only is used for this purpose, woollen cloth has been found ineffectual." Grapes are kept by sealing both ends of the cut bunch with sealing-wax and hanging the bunches on a line in a dry room.

Gooseberries are preserved, before modern bottling methods, by filling bottles, close corking them and sealing the cork with wax, and then burying them in the ground.

In the chapter on fruit trees many varieties of apples are mentioned, some of which may now be forgotten, but their names are like a ring of words, full of the poetry of old orchards.

Smallest curly ripe, margarote apple, golden rennet, golden pippin, nonpareil, large royal russet, grey russet, nonsuch, royal permain, margitle apple, Dutch codlin, aromatic russet, kitchen rennet, cat's head, hanging body, lemon pippin, English rennet, grey Paddington, white costin, stew pippin, kirton pippin, summer and winter queening rambour, white French rennet, summer and winter pomine d'apis, Dutch dwarf paradise and jennetings, with many others.

Cherries have May-duke, Archduke, bleeding heart, carnation, black cordown, white groffian, lukeward, ox heart, white guigne, and the black and red cherries of the hedgerow.

Plums have no Victorias, because the queen was not crowned, but great black damask, earl damask, white permerdian, early Morocco, blue perdrigen, Fotheringhame, blue gage, drapel, grosse queen claude, la mirabelle, red queen mother, brignole plum, diagnenoir, maître clauddaugshing, and many strange old names.

Pears — the list is very long, but I will give a

few names of these lost sweet fruits. Green chissetus, early musk, red muscadelle, little muscat, citron des Carmes, Catherine, orange musk, and the good jargonelle, which has lasted a hundred years. There is summer bon chrétien, musk robin, rose pear, summer bergamotte, golden beurre, green sugar, little russelete, swan egg, grey good wife, messier jean, winter thorn (very buttery), good Lewis of winter, Parkinson's wardens, St. Michael, lambretti, and small winter button, and the great black pear of Worcester.

What a musical list, with its admixture of old French!

Seeds of flowers are collected, lilies are divided, and a general economy is practised which is not practised now with the scores of nurserymen ready to sell their seeds and bulbs. The variety of flowers was limited, the lilies mentioned are the orange lily, the martagon and the crown imperials, but the fruit trees, when there was little imported fruit, were of great importance. There is a long list of kitchen garden plants in this little Gardener's Calendar, with many kinds of melons, beans, peas, gourds, "garlicks" and onions. As one ponders the lists one sees that the kitchen garden and orchard were of vast importance, and the common man was a great gardener, as he still is, for although many of the large gardens have disappeared, there are multitudes of new small gardens, in new towns and villages and "housing" estates, where the old arts are practised and the old love of a kitchen garden remains.

CHAPTER
SIX

Rockeries

No country garden was complete without a rockery, which was not an alpine garden filled with choice flowers from far lands, growing among imported morraines and glaciers, but a collection of rocks with something growing among them, to enhance their own intrinsic beauty of structure. The rocks were the important factor, not the plants, which were secondary and used to emphasize the stone. A rockery was a garden of ancient lineage, dating from prehistoric times. It is curious that this name, rockery has been confused with that of the rock garden and used as a term of reproach. The rockery was often bleak and forbidding in the town garden, when the stones filled a space where nothing would grow, a sunless corner, but in the little country gardens it had such simplicity and *naïveté* that the passer-by was forced to stop and admire, and the lace curtains would part gently at the window as the owner peeped out to see who was attracted by the show.

Many a little rockery was displayed in the cottage gardens for the neighbours' pleasure and the delight of the children, and it was imperative to look at and speak about these small creations of arts and crafts. There was a rockery against the house wall of a cottage in Cheshire, in the narrow strip of soil dividing the cottage from the country road. In such a small space there was room only for a rose tree which grew on the wall

and the rockery which was made for all to share. We had walked across the great park of the Hall, among the shy fallow deer, past the lake, and we came to the village itself with its water wheel and weir and little bridge and the inn, The Swan with Two Necks. Here, in this secluded spot, we found our rockery, and I was taken back to childhood and the pleasures in such normal sights, when I was a peerer at rockeries in many a small garden, an assistant gardener in them too.

This one had fossils collected over the years, from the local rocks, which we could see as we looked closely, and there were stones each of which contained something of interest, an embedded fossil fern, some fossil shells and encrinites, a piece of iron pyrites, a crystal of quartz, a striation in the rock face. Friends had helped to make this collection, they had found a fossil and brought it for the rockery, as richer people might give a rose bush or a lily. The rockery was a private country museum. Among some of the stones grew a blue primrose, also a special plant, and some blue anemones. There was a hart's-tongue fern, a denizen of rockeries, and London Pride, and a shell. A stone quern also had a place among the trophies. All of these had an air, a feeling of pride and English exclusiveness, they were unique in their own small way, and when we saw the curtains move we were glad we had stopped.

One year when we walked that way we were disappointed that some of the fossils had gone. Perhaps the old people had died, and their children had taken the fossils to their own homes. But there was something else, a carved stone head, a relic from the church tower or from a manor house, a head of distinction, with boldly carved lips and jutting brown and slightly sinister face. There were more ferns too, and a scrap of carved stone edging. Many times we have seen pieces of stone carving displayed on cottage rockeries, brought from the churchyard after a fall of stone, or found when renovations were made. Possibly the inhabitant of the cottage was a stone-mason who had repaired a broken boss or an ornament on the church wall, and the odd scraps of carvings were given to him.

In our country villages we kept a lookout for rockeries which always fascinated a child with their treasures displayed for the passer-by. If we gazed with deep longing and we knew the owners, perhaps a small fossil or a piece of coveted granite or limestone would be slipped into our hands and we took it home to our own rockery. I always wished for a carved head, a strange saintly face to put among our own small treasures, but our church had no such trophies.

The correct place for a rockery was behind a water trough where a spring entered. The stones surrounded the source of the spring, keeping it from harm, and ferns and saxifrage grew luxuriantly among these rocks. We looked about for fossils or pieces of gypsum, or rocks with veins of lead, or crystals of quartz, and with hart's-tongue ferns we were content. We returned from journeys carrying heavy stones without a murmur, and we put the specimens behind the troughs, slipping them into place so that they fitted into the picture.

A Buckinghamshire rockery in a village near

Hartwell has some ammonites in their rocky settings, the beautiful fossils which occur in the clay of this district, and they are so large that out of doors is the only place to display them. It is always necessary to look closely at a rockery to find its half-hidden secrets, and not to dismiss it idly as "a heap of old stones".

Some cottages had small objects made of coloured glass or pottery half-hidden among the ferns, objects which would be despised now, but we thought they were beautiful. They were half-concealed by the ferns, so that only their charms were visible, for they were choice ornaments, inherited from the long past and now broken. A china horse snapped off from a Staffordshire group, a Lady Godiva whose arm was lost, a little basket of flowers from a Crown Derby figure, a shepherd from a Dresden piece, cast out by the Hall and picked up by someone from the rubbish heap, the treasures were more exquisite in their new surroundings of fern and rock and green water than they had been on a shelf or table in a drawing-room. They were washed by the spring and by the rain, they shone brightly in their azures and deep purples and faded gold, they were immortal like a fairytale brought to life. They were not common, and nobody had more than one little scrap of china, to be the centre-piece of the rockery, a small gleaming scrap of beauty illuminating the green.

We had none of these ornaments, our rockeries were too sternly made for such frivolities, but I kept the small broken heads among my toys for safety. We were sometimes invited to the rockery of an old farmhouse belonging to a neighbour about a mile away. After tea we walked down the paved paths in the flower-filled garden, past the moss roses and sweet williams and pinks, past the beehives, to a spring which we could hear long before we arrived at its lair. It was a wild and living thing, as it leapt out of the rockery with great force and rushed into the trough for drinking water and out again to an underground channel, from which it was led through the orchard to join a stream and finally the river. We drank from this cold spring, using a china mug which our friends carried. It was a ritual, a visit to the spring, a drink and then the sight to be seen. Like the worshippers at the sacred springs in Greece we went, our hearts uplifted with excitement to see, not a god but a little china shepherd boy.

"Would you like to see the little blue man?" we were asked. It was the desire of life to see him again, a miracle hidden in the ferns. For he was invisible, hidden away from sight. Hands ruffled the ferny fronds and the blue man about four inches high was placed in our own small palms. He had a tricorn hat, and his clothes of the eighteenth century were the brightest blue, like the summer sky. He smiled with his exquisite little face, and we turned him over to see the faded gold buttons at the back of his jacket. Then he was replaced among the ferns and we returned to the house, content. We had seen him, the treasure, and we never noticed the breakage which had banished him to this lonely spot in the rockery nor did we consider it a banishment. It was a great honour to be there, guarding the spring.

We had no broken figurines among our solemn rocks, but there were some strange objects. One was a carved piece of wood, shaped like a primitive man, whose origin I never heard. It had always been there, we would have been told. I never played with it, I had a faint dislike and fear of it. There was a heavy stone ring, and the quern, large stone weights, and a lump of spar containing some Blue John crystals. There were large lumps of spar which had quartz crystals in groups like the towers and transparent castles of a minute fairyland, and there were masses of tufa with ferns in the deep hollows and natural caves of the rock, and deep black veins of lead ran through some of the stone. Every piece was unique in its own beauty. Lichens and golden stonecrops, and starry gems of moss soon embroidered the stones, and little ferns of polypody sprang up in the crannies. There was no need for flowers in these green rockeries by the water troughs, in the yard and garden verges, but primroses grew by the troughs in the fields and clumps of foxgloves seeded there to make a natural rock garden.

These rockeries were in many villages of the north, but they are rarer in the south, except in Devon and Cornwall. Instead the rock garden flourishes, small and neat with its masses of purple aubretia, which we never grew. "White rock" was a rock covering, a flower much loved by the honey bees as it hung from a rock-edged lawn, but no "purple rock". I missed my rockeries, and so I made a little rock garden out of a lavender bed, which was sprawling too much. It was my first adventure in this realm of the small plants, the diminutive and fairy-like flowers about which I was so ignorant.

At first it was an experiment and purple aubretia spread over every inch, so I banished it and began again. The variety of Alpine bulbs astonished me, and the flowers were a revelation of beauty unknown before. I bought many tiny bulbs and looked forward to the discovery of many new flowers, strangers to me. In February came the little tulip, Pulchella Violet Queen, a deep royal purple tulip, very small and close to the ground, the most welcome colour to see on a snowy morning. Snowdrops and aconites were not planted in the rock garden, they had their own quarters. So the tulips in their bishop's mantle and cope grew there, to astonish me. Next came the Fusilier tulips, miniature, but not as minute as the Pulchella, scarlet as soldiers. These two, the Violet Queen and the Fusilier, take the place of the blue boy whom I saw in the rockery of childhood days, for they are treasures, hiding behind rocks, braving the wind and snow, bringing colour to the earth, small as crocuses, but sturdy and valiant. There was no fragility about them, and they lasted a long time. The Prestans Fusiliers with orange-red or scarlet flowers stand up with no nonsense about them, veritable tiny tulips which do not bend or bow to the winds. The Fusilier himself has three flowers on a stalk, a bunch of flowers in one. These were in bloom in April, making a fine colour on the rock garden's edges.

Before these I had a drift, in March, a swarm, a bevy of anemones, Blanda varieties, blue and pink and lavender, all over the garden for I had dropped the corms in odd places and forgotten them. Like the wild anemones, a favourite flower of March in our fields, I saw this lovely wind flower, nodding its tiny beaded head in the breeze, swaying its petticoats of green. I picked bunches to have them in the house, and they went on growing, with the abandon of the wild ones which come up in my little wood. Long ago in a garden I saw a blue sheet of Apennine anemones and I wished to have the same, but mine were of many colours and quite as beautiful.

Every day something new appeared, and I had constant surprises. There were the Alpine crocuses, the Sieberi, soft blue-lavender, very delicate and ethereal, so thin and waif-like I put a cloche over to shield them from the rain lest they dissolved. They were made of sterner stuff than I thought, and they survived. I found the susianus, Cloth of Gold, brown-wood petals with yellow inside, and the snow bunting, which I bought for its name, cream-coloured with feathering like the bird, and the lovely tiny Thomasinianus, Taplow Ruby. Purple, snowy, lilac, striped, these miniature alpine crocuses are fairy-like. They are not for picking for the house, although I cannot resist a few, but they prefer to be out in the cold. The disadvantage of these little crocus varieties is that the mice like the corms and eat them quickly. I had sad losses.

I grew the yellow-hooped petticoat daffodil, quaint and witchlike with its pointed hat, and the Cyclamineus narcissi, another dainty flower with a ruffled-edged trumpet and reflexed perianth, an odd little gem of a flower, which should be grown in large quantities in the grass as I first saw it in the Saville gardens at Windsor. It spattered the grass with gold drops, and it was much more in tune with grass than the larger daffodils. I found it very hardy and resilient; even when somebody trod on the flowers they rose up and smiled again. The minimus is the tiniest of daffodils, and this is more suitable to the rock garden than to grass: it is so small, so perfect a miniature.

The Nanus dwarf daffodil is another treasure, and also the lovely Angel's tears, the triandrus alba. This is a March flower with a cluster of little drops of white, with reflexed petals. The larger variety, Thalia, I grow in the larger garden, for I adore all these white narcissi, and the shape of Thalia is very pure and moving in its delicacy. It reminds me of the snowdrop in winter, in its grace and innocence.

The Erythronium Dens Canis, which has the easier name of dog's tooth violet, is another of the beauties of the rock garden, and I always wish I had seen this in childhood days. I think it is still a wild flower in some other country, perhaps Greece or Sicily; I do not know the origin of this lovely creature. The leaves are marbled with beautiful browns and fawns on the green, and the flowers are divine. They resemble miniature Regale lilies, a fairy lily, with hanging head and reflexed petals and bunch of stamens. They are white, rosy purple, or palest pink. There is no resemblance to a violet and one has to explain this so often. They are more like African violets in their shades of colour. The name of dog's tooth comes from the shape of the roots, a dull name for a lovely flower which carries a hint of enchantment. I think they were in Persephone's bunch when she slipped back to earth from Pluto's kingdom. I should certainly pick them if I were allowed a minute's grace from eternal shade. They have long stalks and they will last well in water, and they look perfect in a wine-glass which reveals their beauty of stalk and flower. I wait for these small flowers as eagerly as I wait for the cuckoo.

Another flower I grow on my rough little rock garden is the ordinary field fritillary, a magical flower beyond all others. Its chequered bell, its strange colour like a gipsy's head scarf, criss-crossed with fine lines and pattern, its slender stems grass-like and the grassy leaves, all make it a flower of distinction. Some are wine coloured, some are chocolate, some are snow white. and some are greenish. They can be grown in grass, or under the shade of trees, but I reserve mine for the rock garden where they are safe from dogs and feet. The tall lily, the Crown Imperial, another fritillary, grows under the wood, in splendour and majesty, but these humble little wild flowers are happier in safety. They have been uprooted and extinguished from many an English meadow, and now they are kept in captivity, or the species might vanish.

The Iris has many variants in miniature, which are a delight to the eye as they grow in the rock garden. The yellow Danfordiae is one I have, deep lemon yellow, showing in February, braving the weather, it grows close to the earth. Reticulata is well known, for it is often grown in the house in bowls to come out in January, and I find it easier in this way than in the garden, where it is diffident with me. It is blue, gentian blue, with narrow tongue, a lovely little flower, with a stalk longer than the Danfordiae. Tuberosa would not flower for me, and others have been reluctant, but some which grow well are unknown by name, irises which have grown so thickly they have had to be transplanted to another place. These were bought in a little shop, dwarf irises, blue and sweet. The most poetical of all the little tulips is the Lady Tulip, Clusiana, with its red-rose and white petals, and its delicate shape. It grows freely, happily, like a wild flower, and it is a good flower for cutting. It is like one of the wild tulips in the paintings by the seventeenth-century Dutch artists. A dainty little yellow tulip, wild from Turkey, is a companion for this. Its petals are short and slightly curved. The Kaufmanniana tulips are another species, which I enjoy very much; green-yellow, or red and white with open flower-heads which give them the name of Waterlily tulips. They are larger than the other species of tulips, because their petals open flat. All of these have very short stalks, and they grow so close to the ground they seem to be floating there. Fritz Kreisler is a good variety, with coral and white petals, and orange tips. Many of these are named after musicians, and one can take one's choice.

Many of these tulips, fritillaries and dog's tooth violets which grow in a rock garden, are unknown to people, who see them for the first time when they peer into the mysteries of stone and closely carpeted ground. Yet they are common enough and cheap enough, and they give the greatest pleasure to the viewer. The tiny cyclamen also grow there, especially the Neapolitan, rose pink and very hardy and prolific. They are gathered to fill tiny glass jugs and wine-glasses, to show their stems and the curving shape of the flowers. I have seen them growing between the great roots of oaks in the Saville gardens, at Windsor, but my trees are beeches and the shade is too dense for these flowers. Gentians of many kinds grew well in my rock garden when first I planted them, but in time they have decreased, and died away, a great sorrow for they were very beautiful and I thought they were secure. Perhaps there was not enough shade for them.

House leek, brought from a cottage roof, and rock roses, the cystus, in many shades of yellow and coral and pink make fine clumps among the stones, covering some of the lesser plants. These have to be ruthlessly cut back, or they would take all the limited space. There are a few miniature roses which have tiny flowers in double white, in red and pink, and there are two little cypress trees about five inches high. Lythospernum grows with reluctance, and it is a flower of such vivid blue I wish I could keep it happy. My rock garden lacks the supreme virtue, the gift of living water flowing through it, and the water-loving plants have a struggle to survive. I think with regret of all the little flowers we might have grown in our rockeries, if we had ever heard of their existence, but this miniature world was unknown to country people in those days. There is no room for bushes, but two grow very well among the bulbs, a snow-white dwarf azalea, called Palestrina, and a small tree of the Praecox rhododendron, a gem of a plant which has lavender flowers full out in March over all the leafless branches. Under it grow blue and mauve primroses, to add to its entrancing beauty. I saw this shrub at the Saville Gardens on an icy March day and at once ordered three for my garden. One grows by the lead statue, one died and the third flourishes in the rock garden. I heard a wise adage once on gardening. "When you order, get three, one to put where you think the plant will grow, one for the place your friends think, and the third for the place it won't grow. The last is the best."

As spring turns to summer, the rock garden has less colour and variety, nor do I struggle to alter this. I enjoy the quiet green after the excitement of spring, and I do not seek to enliven it with any spurious annuals. It rests, waiting for another spring, for February when the first Puchellas come out. The excitement is over, the trunks are packed, the show is done.

At the Chelsea Show the rock gardens are one of the most popular of all the displays in that vast showground of gardeners. Little streams cascade down rocky slopes, they make small fountains as they spray over stones, they drop into little quiet pools, they water the lilies and the spikes of primulas and rushes which cunningly grow in the grass verges. It is a miracle of beauty.

They are so natural, so easy to understand, so delicate in their crystal purity that there is always an admiring crowd pressed against the rails like spirits outside Paradise. I feel so homesick when I hear that tinkle of water and see those streams, I nearly weep. Each one of us imagines a waterfall in his own patch of garden, rising unbidden from the earth, and some of us see the hills behind and hear the bleat of sheep and the cry of birds in the uplands. So we stand and stare and dream of the waterfalls we know, in hilly lands far away, and we feel cut off from our own country where such things are natural.

A few people are more practical and they ask questions about the pump which forces the water upward, but we are all enchanted by the beauty of the rock gardens and the running stream. One garden has rocks of Westmorland stone, and one has blocks of rich red sandstone, and the masses of stone give a pang to the heart of the stone-lover. Golden stonecrops grow among the rocks naturally, and the crannies of stones are cunningly filled with tiny plants. Water buttercups, the Mayblobs are there in the water, and arrow head and primulas.

These are the perfect rock gardens, besides which all our efforts are puny, but they are man-made. Once I saw a perfect rock garden, on the side of a fell in Yorkshire. A stream ran down Waddington Fell, bouncing over the rocks, singing, leaping, a wild little torrent, but very small. It ran through the garden of a large old house, and the owners had guided the little wild creature to pools, and planted masses of the most delightful flowers, which were akin to the water, so that the blue gentians, the tiny ferns, the rock roses and all the brave company of alpines were in their true setting, growing in a luxuriance which I have never seen equalled in any garden in the south. It was one of the things to remember for life, beauty beyond compare, but wars have passed over the land and I do not know whether the rock garden still exists. Soon Nature takes a hand, and the stream becomes a torrent, the plants are torn away, and only the dream remains.

The plants disappear, the rocks are torn up and tossed together, and the beginning of a rockery is made as life turns a full circle.

Strange pang of conscience for the weed, whose beauty
None celebrates, and for the stone imprisoned
In one poor form, deprived of growth and movement
Loveless, unhonoured.

CHAPTER
SEVEN

Dolls and
their Houses

Dolls are universal toys, the small replicas of human beings, nursed by the young of many countries and many civilizations, figures whose origin is steeped in magic and religion, but perhaps in modern days there is too much stress on their place in the fertility cult. For it seems to me that the young of the human race, like the young of all animals, have played and found something to amuse themselves with in the happy days of extreme youth, and a doll, like a ball, can be made out of the simplest materials.

A child of the poor plays with a wooden spoon decked out with a handkerchief, or she nurses a small log dressed up in a shawl, and the facial resemblance to a human being is not essential to the imaginative mind which can see life in every single thing.

Greek and Roman children played with dolls, and some little dolls have been found in the catacombs. Dolls were the toys of the ancient Egyptians, and the Red Indian babies (austere infants who never cried), had dolls to play with, small wooden creatures, like themselves swathed in cocoons. Dolls were of course made to represent human beings for witchcraft purposes, but the chief use was for amusement, for companionship.

Among the most primitive people dolls were common objects, and it is interesting to conjecture their materials. Dolls are made from bones, or from rough pieces of wood, such as we found and made into dolls, for the small knotted twigs of the oak and the smooth-warmed white sycamore made delicate dolls of character. Flat stones with a face chalked upon the surface, little boulders, smooth and neat, farm implements and kitchen gear, especially wooden spoons and potato mashers, all could be dressed as dolls and nursed and trundled about by the owner. There was more vitality in these improvised dolls than in a wax-faced model from a shop.

The dolls had to live in dolls' houses, and again the variety depended upon the child and the century and the civilization. So it is probable that an early dolls' house was a tiny wigwam, a straw mat in a bush, or a hollow in the side of the cave. Caves make the best dolls' houses, with their natural shapes, their finished curves and their safety from marauding animals.

The word doll has been confused with the word "idol", and although there is no connection there may have been confusion in the minds of evangelical people. The figures of the saints in churches were attacked as idols in the time of the reformation, and even now representation of saints by small figures is disliked by some people on religious grounds. I heard a sermon against idols when I was young, and I was so deeply impressed I thought it referred to my own doll. This was a primitive wooden doll which had belonged to generations before me, an inherited doll of long lineage, smooth as silk with caressings, legless and armless and hairless, a magical being, and I was aware she had powers. She might rise up in the night and smite me, and I wrapped her in a shawl and kept her down in my bed, where her heavy body comforted me in the dark. No other doll had this resemblance to an idol. She had a Mona Lisa smile, very beautiful and benign, and her cheeks were smooth and soft. Even her flat nose was gentle, she had an occult life, and she was an idol who had to go.

The word "doll" was given by old country people to a baby's hand and wrist. I remember, before I could speak, being told to keep my "dollies" in bed, and my small fists were placed under the coverlet. "Hold out thy dolly," someone would say and I held out my hand. This old custom and this use of the word must relate to the resemblance of the fist to a doll's head. In some childish games the adult dresses her hand in a handkerchief and mimes with the "dolly", while a song is chanted, as in:

"O Father Kelly, I've come to confess."
"Well, Daughter Bridget, and what is amiss?"
"O Father Kelly, I've killed the cat."
"Well, Daughter Bridget, there's nothing in that."

The dressed-up hand was a puppet, a person come to life in miniature, and we stared entranced at this doll-play.

Dolls were costume figures, elegant creatures, in Queen Anne's days and in Georgian days, when they were dressed to exhibit clothes as if they were mannequins. Lately this custom has been revived and in a recent exhibition in London there were dolls dressed in the latest fashions, completely finished from their spectacles and sunglasses to their gilded sandals, handbags and high-heeled shoes. Exquisite human beings with piled up hair and their powder cases, they were about a foot high, a grown-up toy and not for children.

In the eighteenth and nineteenth centuries children were often painted with their dolls, and very charming these dolls are with their bonnets and sashes, their feathered hats and their stiff boots, as they are held tightly to the child's breast. Many a portrait has been made delightful by the presence of a doll, and the happiness in the child's face.

The word "doll" was not in common use at this period, "Children's baby" was used instead, and doll-makers were called "Children's baby-makers". A dolls' house was a "Baby-house", and the well-known and beautiful house, was the "Westbrook Baby-house". Hand-embroidered carpets of the time of Queen Anne are on the floors of this treasure, the ladies have powdered hair, and the winding staircase is lighted by a lantern dome. This is now in the Bethnal Green Museum, and it is dated 1760.

In a corner cupboard, between the stuffy dark pantry with its shelves of jam and candles, and the cool light dairy with its bowls of cream, tucked in the passage way was the doll's house. Nobody would have suspected that a genteel family lived in that narrow, ancient, three-cornered cupboard, painted cream like the walls, an integral part of the house, immovable as the rock upon which the house was built.

There were really two cupboards, the upper one stored with china, with breakfast cups and saucers, with jugs and plates on its cornered shelves, but the lower cupboard was given to me, as the home of my dolls. The top cupboard reached to the ceiling, and we had to get a stool to lift articles from the top shelf which was the medicine store, ready for any emergencies of a house far from the doctor. There, safe from prying fingers, were pills and ointments, herbs and embrocations. The lower cupboard was so close to the ground people had to kneel on the doormat to look into it. It had been the candlestick cupboard for many years, a dusty place where the antique iron candlesticks, long hand-made slips of iron on round bases, and the tin candlesticks for workmen and servant boy were kept. None of the beautiful brass and

pewter candlesticks were there. It was the store-room for very old primitive ironware which we had inherited from other days. The contents of that cupboard would be in a museum nowadays, but we got rid of the old iron, and the cupboard was scrubbed and given to me. I was elated. Two of the three-cornered shelves were the doll's house sitting-room and the bedroom. I sat on the doormat arranging the rooms, spreading out my furniture, making carpets for the floors from paper, putting treasures of feather and flower seed on the paper plates, and in the little vases, in the house of the candlesticks.

Nobody could disturb this doll's house, mice could not enter, and people would not notice it. Before this I had a sugar-box, papered and painted to make a house, but it was too large and clumsy, and I was always in somebody's way when I played.

When the mice found my sugar-box house and visited the open rooms to nibble the dolls' food I was thankful to get the candle cupboard for its privacy. The dolls themselves were the penny dolls we bought at the village from the newspaper shop, and their size was in proportion to the neat small furniture. They seemed to fit into the life of flowers and berries and shells we brought indoors for the decoration of the candle house.

Recently at an exhibition of flower decorations at the R.H.S. in Westminster, I saw a small house which reminded me of our little doll's house. It was made in an oak cupboard, and each shelf was a small room with antique furniture. There were no inhabitants for it was the background for a display of miniature flowers — the tiny roses and buds and berries of dwarf plants, arranged in little vases no larger than thimbles, were set on the dolls' tables and dresser. The whole was so enchanting that a cord had to be placed in front to keep people from crowding around it. Tiny woven baskets were filled with diminutive flowers as if some small elf had been to a garden to fill them for the Show. The dining-table was set with little knives and forks and plates and in the centre of the table was a pot of miniature blossoms all in proportion to the room. Realism can go very far in a dolls' house and imagination is a precious commodity. Real smoke rises from the dolls' house chimney, the staircase with hand-rail has a carpet which covers it neatly and softens the footfall of the dolls going to bed. A violin which lies on a table might play if one touched the strings, and silvery music might come from the shrouded harp in the corner of the room. A key might turn in the lock of the door, a lamp might be lighted, as it was lighted in imagination in the little doll's house which Katherine Mansfield describes so poignantly.

"All the rooms were papered. There were pictures on the walls, painted on the paper, with gold frames complete. Red carpet covered all the floors except the kitchen; red plush chairs in the drawing-room, green in the dining-room, tables, beds with real bed-clothes, a cradle, a stove, a dresser with tiny plates and one big jug. But what Kezia liked more than anything, what she liked frightfully, was the lamp. It stood in the middle of the dining-room table, an exquisite little amber lamp with a white globe. It was even filled ready for lighting, though of course you couldn't light it. . . . The lamp was perfect. It seemed to smile at Kezia, to say 'I live here'. The lamp was real."

So each object becomes alive, and it doesn't matter that the lamp cannot be lighted, the imagination makes a flame and warms the fingers at the golden globe and the red paper fire.

Once I came across a dolls' house set out in a Yorkshire lane, in the country far from a village. There was a sycamore tree growing on a primrose-covered bank, and the house was made under this tree. A doormat of coarse fibre and a red plush plaque with a picture of a robin made the parlour in front of the tree. The kitchen, built in the bare arching roots of the tree, had a spade head for a stove. There was no doubt of this, the head and the handle stuck in the earth were the framework of a kitchen range. Little hollows in the trunk of the tree made cupboards, for the sycamore always has little cupboards for children to discover and fill. Steps on the bank up in the curving roots led to a bedroom on the grassy field above the bank. A handkerchief lay drying on the bushes in the tree's own garden of primroses. Hawthorn, holly, primroses and anemones with pale willow saplings made the house's surroundings, its orchard, garden and croft. Robins and chaffinches were singing in the tree, as if they enjoyed the make-believe of the children who were invisible to me. I have never forgotten this wayside shrine of a house, in this far away green land.

The famous dolls' house made by Sir Neville Wilkinson is called "Titania's Palace". I saw this fairytale dwelling which has an element of human magic in its construction, at a time when I still possessed my cupboard house. I admired it, but I felt it was disconcerting in its realism. There is sufficient fantasy in a dolls' house without the addition of invisible fairies, whose wings are kept in a cupboard. Old Bristol glass is in the dining-room, Titania's piano is ready for music, landscapes painted in 1650 by Molenaer hang on the walls. These pictures were painted for a Dutch child long ago, and collected for this fairy dolls' house. Bedrooms and nurseries for the baby Prince, all are perfection of beauty and rarity and all have a unique quality.

Neville Wilkinson's palace is furnished with many antique pieces, for their collection has gone on for generations, and people have hunted everywhere for these rare objects. One interesting thing is a cannon, dated about 1590, and this may have been a model of a cannon, to be shown as a specimen of work, a traveller's sample. Miniature merchandise was carried as traveller's samples in the days when highwaymen and outlaws infested the roads. So these small replicas of articles fulfilled a useful purpose for advertisement and sale to customers, and probably they were much desired by the merchant's children.

A miniature set of chairs was displayed in the office of a famous chair factory at High Wycombe, Buckinghamshire; the chairs had been made recently as samples. I possess a small bureau of the time of Queen Anne, a miniature which is perfect in every detail, with walnut shell, and inlay and tiny drawers which slide like silk and little brass handles. This was a sample made by a firm of wood workers and craftsmen of Queen Anne's reign.

The Queen's Dolls' House, which is exhibited at Windsor Castle, is a house of miniatures made by craftsmen with many objects specially made for the house. The china was manufactured by Doulton, the chairs were carved by living artists. In the library the two hundred books were written by authors in their own hand-writing; one of them, "The haunted doll-house", by the ghost-tale writer, M. R. James.

In the kitchen there is a miniature knife-machine, already old-fashioned, and a mincing machine. The bathroom has an alabaster bath with silver taps which turn, and the floor of the little room is mother-of-pearl. The pictures in the house are painted by well-known artists, and there is a music library of fifty volumes of music by contemporary British composers, each just over an inch in size, bound in leather. They were photographed and reduced in size from real volumes.

Every house for dolls seems to be magnificent and glorious, in contrast to a little house I once saw by the sandy path in a Cheshire wood. It had been made by playing children and left when they went home for tea, with regret, I am sure.

It was constructed within the roots of a great oak tree with bare arching roots washed by the rains. It was surrounded by a fence of twigs about an inch high, evenly spaced, and this palisade was a work of art itself. Infinite toil must have gone to the work, it was so neat. Acorns were the cups and saucers in the little rooms, and beech mast was the food, stored in a larder made in the tree's roots. There were tiny dishes made of bark, and the viands came from the hedgerows, berries and nuts and buds of flowers. Little beds were made of twigs slim and brown, laid like mattresses between bedposts which were larger twigs stuck in the sandy soil. Flat silvery pieces of shale made tables and a long flat silvery table stood in the middle of the room with tiny round pebbles as seats. Everything had been chosen and made with the seeing eye of an imaginative child, and everything was part of the earth, a natural object found in the woodland. A child of the Old Stone Age might have made such a house, for it was eternally part of childhood.

CHAPTER
EIGHT

Witches

When we crept softly through the woods, keeping on the soft places between the stones, making our zigzag way without a word, we were placating the witches which haunted the dark places, which were prepared to leap out at us at nightfall. Nobody told us about witches, we knew without any speech, and when we heard the story of Hansel and Gretel who wandered through a wood such as ours and found a cottage in the depths we expected to find the same little house made of ginger-bread crisp and golden, with sugar plums on the roof and almond rock on the roof. We knew we couldn't resist such dainties, we should eat and be captured. There was no escape from witches except the sign of the cross. I did not discover this talisman until I was older, for we were an evangelical family. When I went to school I met my first witch. She was an old woman in a red shawl and she muttered to herself as she walked along the country road.

"Run! Run!" cried the children. "She's a witch! She will catch you and take you home and eat you."

So I ran faster than I had ever run before, and I expected the witch to fly on wings after me. Nothing happened, but I kept a wary eye for her. She could change me into a cat or a fox or a hare I was told, and I believed this.

All this was secret, unknown to parents, a strange legend which passed from infant mouth to infant mouth, a tale of witchcraft, come down through the centuries. It must be true, I argued to myself. It was in a book, my fairy tale book, and in a poem by Burns I heard, and all books and poems were gospel truth. A witch could put a little girl in a circle, and there was no getting free from that boundary. In daytime I did not mind, I rather enjoyed the excitement of running from a witch, but at night it was different. A witch had flaming eyes and she could see when I could distinguish nothing. She lay in wait in my bedroom, behind the door on a winter's night. She clothed herself in a dressing-gown or a petticoat, which hung on the door, and she waited for me to close my eyes. I could see her eye glint in the light of the fire. In the morning she was only a brass hook on the door but that was her changed shape, her deceitful concealment from grown-up people. They said she was a hook; I knew she was a witch and laughter would not dissuade me. I did not talk about her for this gave her extra power over me.

There were witches in the Bible, and I heard of them in Church where I felt safe and content. The Witch of Endor, whom I saw with a pointed hat on her grey hair, carrying a wand, which she turned to the ground, to summon up the spirits of the dead. Dark glittering eyes, curved chin and nose, and quick nervous voice belonged to a witch, a skinny hand and claws for fingers. Adults did not speak of witches, they said they did not exist nowadays, but once upon a time it was different. Then they told strange tales, which would be explained now by psychology, a split personality, hypnotism, good and evil lurking in one body, a psychopath.

Science seeks for unity in nature, laws obeyed by forces, mathematical exactitude in the play of behaviour, and witches who work against known laws will not be tolerated. Yet I think there was some potent reason for the belief in witches, which was current until a century ago. The belief is still alive, say some people who pry into old superstitions and seize on haphazard careless talk by the older country people. This talk is then held up to ridicule, and disdain. "We who know better than they", is an attitude of ignorance. It should be "We do not know, we cannot explain such things by any known laws, but the world changes, and new laws are discovered which may throw a light on these strange happenings in the future." For the superstitions of one era are the science of another.

The power of the evil eye was well-known among primitive races and the power was practised in this land also. It cannot be measured in any scientific manner, in any known units of force. It doubtless has a psychological name; the owner of the power no longer puts a spell on somebody to influence him unduly, even to bring illness and death, but he exerts an influence through the mind. Telepathy is now accepted, and this may have been the means of power in the reputed witch.

The punishment for witchcraft was death by burning and this cruel penalty seems to have been exploited to get rid of many innocent victims. Many thousands were burnt in a few years, but there must have been some strong reason which we do not know for the strength of the powers of sorcery. More might be discovered in a study of the powers of magic among primitive people.

Recently I went into an antique shop in a small Cotswold village to enquire my way. On a table lay a large thin book, beautifully bound, in a tooled leather, and it attracted my attention. I opened it, expecting it to be a religious book, and I was right. It was a long sermon, or series of sermons, published in 1613, and the subject was one that would attract a big congregation if it were preached in a modern church. The title of the book was *A Discourse of the Damned Art of Witchcraft, so farre forth as it is revealed in the Scriptures, and manifest by true experience*. It was "framed and delivered in his ordinarie Course of Preaching by Mr. William Perkins, and published by Thomas Pickering, Batchelor of Divinitie and Minister of Finchingfield, Essex".

It was printed by the "Universitie of Cambridge 1613", but the sermon was preached in 1606, probably as a series of sermons, which must have attracted a good deal of attention in those early years of the reign of James I, a notorious hater of witchcraft and a believer in the powers of witches. So I bought the book and took it home with me, holding it timidly as if I felt something might come out of its brown pages.

Many books have been written about witches since this early one, with statistics of the number of people burned for practising the evil art. The belief still exists in primitive countries, where the "evil eye" of a man can cause another to die and modern doctors can seldom overcome the poor victim's acquiescence in this power, but in civilized lands tolerance, together with discoveries of psychological variations in human behaviour, has removed the scourge or cured it, by hospital treatment, and the definition of witch has changed.

The author of this book defines a witch as a

"Magician who either by open or secret forces, wittingly and willingly consenteth to use the aid and assistance of the Devill in the working of wonders". The wonders are still here, with many more added to them, but the Devil is not invoked, for his power is discredited — which may be a good thing and may not. Witches were the worshippers of Satan, "the Prince of this world, the Murtherer from the beginning" says the preacher, to whom the evil spirit was very real, as indeed he was even in my childhood, although he was always called by his other name, Satan.

This book, dedicated to the Right Honourable Sir Edward Cooke, Lord Chief Justice, was written to show how skilfully the Devil works, in the exercise of the cursed art of Witchcraft. Even the "great clarks" of Greece — Thales, Plato, and others, for want of a better light "sought among the Wizzards of Egypt, whom they called Prophets, men instructed by Satan in the art of Divination. The Magicians of Persia, the ancient Romans, were followers of Satan." It was also the case of Saul and Nebuchadnezzar in the Bible, men who sought knowledge from forbidden sources. "That Witches may and doe work wonders, is proved," he says, "however not by an omnipotent power but by the assistance of Satan the Prince, who is a powerful Prince, yet a Creature, such as they." Thales predicted a solar eclipse, using Babylonian knowledge, hence he was a suspect 2,000 years later.

"After the ascension of Christ into heaven, in the time of Claudius Caesar, the Devil stirred up sundry persons who by the help of "Magic and Sorcerie" were accounted as Gods, and their statues erected and worshipped with reverence. Among the rest was Simon Magus." But Christ locked and bound Satan for 1,000 years after his ascension, that he might not be generally powerful in seducing the Gentiles. Towards the expiration of those years Satan began to renew his kingdom.

"Badde witches and good ones exist," says he, and the good witch uses her powers to unbind the influence of the bad witches. She is equally evil, for she could persuade and seduce people by her powers. The Wise-woman of the village is a witch, he says, sourly, and he has nothing to add in favour of these poor women who have tried in their own way to restore health and sanity. His first tempter in the beginning was Eve, a woman. With Puritan ardour he would root out all of them, and weed the earthly fields clean.

The preacher says there are more women than men witches, because women are more easily persuaded, "the devill hath more easily prevailed on women," and he quotes a Hebrew proverb, "The more women, the more witches".

To discover a witch certain acts were performed. To scratch a witch, to burn the thatch of her house, to bind her and cast her in the water to see if she sank or swam, all these he condemns, not from pity but because a true witch might escape with the Devil's aid. The ignorant people with a rage against an innocent victim could do her harm by suggesting witch-craft, he allows, and the innocent party might be grievously harmed, but he advocates burning for witchcraft, as only fire could remove the great peril. This is surprising, for burning could not destroy the soul, and he believed in the immortality of the soul.

Witches were a scourge, and they were frequent in Spain, Italy, France, Germany, in Elizabethan days and earlier, for the evil of witchcraft was spread through many countries.

England had not the record of other lands in this dire persecution, for the strong individuality kept the courts saner. John Evelyn notes in 1692, "Unheard-of stories of the universal increase in witches in New England; men, women and children devoting themselves to the devil, so as to threaten the subversion of the government.

"Some of the accused were convicted and executed, but Sir Philip Phipps, the Governor had the good sense to reprieve and afterwards pardeon, several; and the Queen approved his conduct." This further note is from the papers of the Rev. John Miller, Chaplain of the King's forces in the Colony.

The preacher in this book on witchcraft goes on to classify kinds of witchcraft, and Divination is one of the accursed arts used by the witches. All who consult an oracle are condemned, all who consult the stars, and all who consult fortune-tellers of any kind, whatever the circumstances.

"Alexander the Great before he made warre with Darius, king of Persia, consulted with the Oracle, that is with the Devill, touching the event and the issue of his enterprise." The answer was "Alexander shall be a conqueror" and he accepted this prophecy and acted upon it, to conquer Asia. "How did the Devill know the future?" asks the preacher. Because this prophecy was mentioned in Daniel, and he used it for his own devices. Sometimes the Devil and the witches know the answers through "their own exquisite knowledge of all naturall things, the influences of the starres, the kinds, vertues and operations of plants, roots, herbs, which knowledge is deeper than that of man, deeper than the knowledge of Philosophers and Doctors".

This statement seems to show an early enmity between church and scientific research, for all advanced knowledge could be dubbed "Witchcraft" by the church, and the spread of pure knowledge was retarded in the name of the Bible.

Some devils attend meetings and gatherings,

hearing what is secretly said and taking the knowledge for their own uses, he adds. "For Satan is agile, he can pass through the world in a moment of time, for God made Satan a spirit."

"The power of Satan, as it was great by his own creation, is able to shake the earth, and to confound the creatures inferior to him in nature and in condition, if he were not constrained by the power of God. So Satan is enabled to do strange works. Strange I say to man, whose knowledge since the fall is mingled with much ignorance, even in natural things whose experience is of short continuance, whose agilitie by reason of his grosse nature is nothing."

Divination is one of the arts of witchcraft, by which the future can be foretold. Divination can be by the true creatures of God, birds flying, and by the noise and the direction they may divine things to come. Jesus himself used divination when he spoke of the winds and clouds. "When you see a cloud rising out of the west, straightway you say, a shower cometh." This is accepted as spiritual because it is a natural happening of nature, such as is known to mariners, farmers. The preacher goes on to some common types of divination which do not differ materially from signs still used by ordinary men in our days. "A man finds a peece of yron, he presently conceived a prediction for some good luck unto himself that daye."

This simple divination later became the charm

attached to a horseshoe, which brought good luck when found, but the horseshoe is not mentioned by the preacher.

"If he light on a peece of silver, then he stands contrarily affected, imagining some evill will befall him." This differs from the superstition of our time, and when I found a silver sixpence lying in the grass by my road only a few days ago, I thought, "Here's a lucky sixpence," as I picked it up and looked at the date, but divination was far from my mind.

Again, "when a man is taking of his journey, if a hare crosse him in the way, al is not well, his journey shal not be prosperous, it presages some mischief to him". This feeling about the innocent hare is still regarded as an omen but it is so rare that it is a delight for the traveller to meet a hare.

"Let his ears tingle and burne, hee is

persuaded he hath enemies abroad, and that some man either then or presently will speake ill about him." This old saying was prevalent among children of my childhood, and people still use it as a kind of thought-transference.

"When the raven stands upon some high place, looke what way he turns himself, and cries, thence, as some thinke, shall shortly come a dead corps." Ravens still carry ill-omen, but their rarity makes them a welcome sight.

"If salte fall toward a man at table, it portendeth (in common conceit) ill news." Again this is a well-known omen still accepted among some, indignantly denied in others, but treated with amusement. The preacher vehemently denies all truth to these vain ideas. "For the truth is they have no vertue in themselves to foreshewe anything that is to come, either by nature or by God's ordinance," says he truly indeed.

"The third kind of creatures used to divine by are the starres," said the preacher. "Divination by starres is commonly called 'Judiciall Astrologie'. This is used by Astrologers, Magicians, Soothsayers, and all proceeds from the Devill."

He continues, "Here if it be thought strange that predictions by so excellent creatures as the starres be, should carry both the name and nature of diabolical practices, which can be done by none as are in league with Satan —" and he gives reasons for the evil work. Divinations by stars are set down by Chaldeans, and Egyptians, but they are only functions of the brain of man.

He concludes. "The Starres are admirable creatures of God and the cause of many strange effects upon the earth, also, so could they not be used in Divination? Now, we grant the Starres and especially the Sunne and the Moone have great vertue and force upon the creatures that are below, partly by their light, and partly by their heat, but hence it will not follow that they may be used for divination."

He discusses the divine elements of the stars which was the belief in those days, and the effects of the Seven Planets, and he takes the signs of the Zodiac and disallows any relation to men born in the different spheres of their influence.

Newton was not born, and the science of astronomy was in its infancy in this country. Astrology was studied as a science, and he braved displeasure with his attack on this subject. Many beliefs of those days are exposed in this sermon, and the faith placed by doctors in astrology. Blood-letting is mentioned. St. Stephen's Day was commonly chosen as a good day for blood-letting, but he refuses to agree. The choice of days, too, by which some are lucky and some unlucky is attacked, and this superstition still prevails. To hunt, to pare the nails, to cut the hair, all had their inauspicious days. The populace who listened to this sermon shook in their shoes as their every-day practices were trounced and the preacher told them that the Devil by these practices takes a stronger hold on the people and gets better acquaintance with them, leading them on to evil.

Divination by dreams is discussed, yet this foretelling of the future is only to be condemned in part. There are three kinds of dreams, he says — Divine, Natural and Diabolical. In the Divine dreams God manifests his will to man and leads him. The dreams of Joseph and of Pharaoh are in this category. Natural dreams are those which arise out of thoughts, the affections of the heart, of the dreamer. A warlike man dreams warlike dreams. The man whose dreams are joyful and pleasant, with mirth and pastime, he is of sanguine complexion. Dreams must not be used to foretell things or they will lead the dreamer into familiarity with the Devil.

The last kind of Divination is "by Lotts", when man casts a die or opens a book to search out his fortune. Such practices he says, are very common. There are three kinds of Lotts, the Civill, the Sporting and the Divining Lott. The Civill is used for the ending of controversy, the dividing of land or heritage, the trying of the right of doubtful things, the discovery of a malefactor hiding among many. (This throws a lurid light upon legal practices of those seventeenth century days.) The Sporting Lott is used to set up bankrupts. The Divining Lott cannot be done without the "confederacy" of the Devil.

Witchcraft in operation is the working of strange wonders, and there are two parts, "Inchantments and Jugling". Here we seem to come to the affairs of a good circus, where these matters are well known in our days, but it is not so.

"The wonders of Inchantments are, the raising of storms, and tempests, winds and weather, by sea or land. The poisoning of the aire" (and here we are truly damned in our time). "Blasting of corne. Killing of cattel and annoying of women and children. Casting out of devills, Such things do Inchanters do." Spells and charms are cast by them.

"Jugling is the delusion of the eye, with some strange sleight of hand done above the ordinary course of nature." Some of these acts were performed by the Jugglers of Egypt, when they turned Aaron's rod into a serpent. Moses also did the same miracles, but theirs were delusions. "The Devill cannot make a real creature," he adds.

So the jugglers were banned in the name of Witchcraft, and one sees the great dangers that attended the wandering players, the jugglers and conjurors at the fairs, the ordinary skilful artists of that time, who practised no magic beyond their own quick sight and touch. The fire-eaters and sword-swallowers, the tricksters and animal tamers, all had to be ready to flee when the eye of the church turned upon them.

The manifestations of the human mind were not understood, and the possessors of any individual gifts were suspected of being under the influence of the Devil. Not for over three hundred years were the visions of the subconscious mind explored scientifically, and the serious work of psychology begun. Mental healing was synonymous with witchcraft, and the wise woman whose hands could cure was preached against in the pulpit, as were those who used subconscious powers to pervert. The influence of mind over matter was probably stronger then than it is now, but it was thought to proceed from the Devil whatever its result. The healing of the mind acts upon the body and brings healing there too. Healers today, are recognized as helpers in hospitals as well as in private practice. I remember some of these healers to whom country people went for help, those whose hands had a touch of power, bringing health and peace to the sick and lonely. They were not regarded as witches, but as saintly women, and they refused payment for their work.

Much of the witchcraft with which people were accused would now be explained by telepathy, by hypnotism, by influences through the mind, for good or evil, by hysteria or hallucinations. Yet there are cases of demoniacal possession even today, when malignant demons or forces seem to take possession of a body, and there are exorcisms to treat this affliction. The deeper levels of consciousness have to be explored and the powers lying in those depths considered. The two strata of consciousness are accepted and it is thought that all human experience, the genius or the evil, lies in the deeper layer where nothing is forgotten and where there is contact with a universal consciousness.

In spite of these scientific explanations, one can easily feel the presence of the old witches, when, in a gale the trees bend down to sweep the ground with skinny fingers, and faces appear in the great trunks of sycamore and beech, when the wind hurls itself round the walls of the house, and screeches like a company of demons, crying, wailing like a lost soul beating with small fists against windows and doors. Then the witches come alive again, and I am a child listening, waiting to be caught and carried off.

CHAPTER
NINE

The Lilies

The lilies-of-the-valley are nearly over and the half-wild lilium pyrenaicum is in flower in the rough bank under the shade of the woodland. It bends its lily heads with the yellow petals streaked with green and the striking scarlet anthers, and I always hurry out in the morning to look at this favourite flower. The petals are neatly curled back as if fresh from the tongs of a woodland hairdresser, and five or six flowers are pendant from each ruffled green stalk.

I brought a few bulbs from my Cheshire garden, twenty years ago, when I came to Buckinghamshire, to remind me of the small square enclosed plot where these lilies grew in quantities under a hedge. The lilies had already been in this wild untended Cheshire garden for many years before we went there, for they were the only plants that remained. I tried to displace them but they would not go, so I let them spring up among the rose bushes. At the last minute when the furniture vans were filled, ready for my departure south, I dug up a few bulbs and thrust them in with the furniture. They were reluctant to grow in Buckinghamshire, they were too hot, too thirsty for a southern county. They pined for their Cheshire habitat. They had leaves in green rosettes, but no flower heads, no drooping yellow curls and orange stamens to powder my cheek and fingers. So I moved the lilies to a dark corner, much shaded by an oak, on the edge of the wood. "Live or die," said I, and they lived.

They have a strong odour which some people find too pungent and overpowering. My little maid always grumbled at the "stink" as she dusted my room which contained the flowers. To me it is a ravishing smell, queer and strange, and I breathe it in as if it were a Basque folk song sung in a rich dark voice at night in a Pyrenees village, far from civilization.

These yellow Turk's cap lilies grew wild in some part of Devon where they were recorded in 1880, but they may have now vanished. I imagine it is an escape from pre-Reformation monasteries, where the monks had grown it for their own medicinal uses. It is so strong growing, so robust in its habits that when well-rooted it spreads rapidly. Solomon's Seal grows near the lilies, and this again is an old plant much used medicinally in the past. The two need the same woodland shade, and their striking flowers seem to illuminate the darkness.

A girl in a village near my Buckinghamshire home gathered some Pyrenaicum lilies, from a field where they had probably been planted by the owner and she took them to the cottage where her baby brother lay. Her mother was out but the neighbour who was in charge cried out in alarm when she saw the magnificent flowers. "You'll poison the baby. Those flowers give out poison in the air, and the baby will die if you don't take them away at once," she was warned.

So the child hurriedly removed the lilies and tearfully awaited her mother, who luckily did not agree about the venomous air, but there is a strong repulsion to the flowers. My little Scottie, Hamish, loved the smell of these lilies. He rose up on his hind legs and put his nose to the lily flowers, sniffing the odour. He went from one clump to another savouring the strong perfume. He was similarly affected by the smell of the golden-brown fragrant wall-flower, which we called by its old name "gilly-flower". He used to stand on his hind legs to sniff at a jug of these flowers on a low table.

Madonna lilies, the Lilium candidum, are easy to grow in most gardens, although they are subject to disease. In cottage gardens they grow richly in the narrow beds under the windows, and they are the only big lily for some people. They never seem to reach the luxurious prodigality of those white gleaming flowers which are the pride of the cottagers. What was the secret of the splendid growth? I think it was the family feeling of the cottage, the sensitivity of the flowers to admiration and love of those who look after them, who tended them with care, watering them, and cherishing them as if they were children. My own Madonna lilies decrease instead of increasing with the years, although I have intense pleasure as I sit by the fragrant tall Madonnas.

My favourite lily, after lily-of-the-valley, is Speciosum, a crimson spotted lily with curving petals of great beauty, embossed with colour as if embroidered. I find it the most rewarding lily, for it blooms late in the year when most flowers are over in my garden. I have many an anxious moment over it, as I watch its long striped buds slowly opening and I listen for the broadcast on frost warnings. If there is a forecast of intense frost I cut a lily and bring it indoors, and cover up the rest for the night. The buds open inside the house, very slowly uncurling their long petals and turning them up one by one until the complete flower is displayed with its golden bunch of stamens. It is an unending pleasure to watch a Speciosum open its slender buds, as if revealing a marvel, and the lily seems to grow even stronger when it is brought indoors. The flowers last into December with the petals complete and perfect. It is the easiest lily to grow and quite the best here.

Some of the Speciosum bulbs were planted, as an experiment, under a beech tree, in a little sloping border which was shaded by the beech but sheltered from the north winds. The flowers opened very late; they did not get enough sun in the summer as the thick leafage of the beech tree was heavy over them. I thought I had made a stupid mistake in this position, but when the beech leaves fell in late October the lilies grew fast in the thin sunshine, the buds expanded and opened. They were not in full flower until November but the flowers were of a richer hue than those in full sun, they were stronger and even more beautiful. There were many lilies on each stem when they came into full flower. I decided to get more Speciosum for this shady woodland place where the stems have to grow slanting to reach the sun, and the lilies open alluring, shy, under the bare trees.

Regale lilies, which were planted in this border did not grow well, for the trees were in leaf and the lilies were shaded. I moved these to a sunnier border. Pardilinum, the scarlet panther lily is easy to grow and it is an enchanting sight like a flame in the green shade. The Hansonii lily, a yellow Martagon, bright yellow and gold, was planted among the roses, but it overtops them and is a robust lily with many reflexed flowers. The Testaceum Excelsum lily is a delicate apricot, a tall lily whose petals are beautiful with their softer colour. This grows in a bed facing west, as an experiment, and it does well in the shaded place.

Little scarlet Tenuifolium Pumilum lilies are planted here and there, but they do not care for the shaded spots under the trees, and I think the squirrels eat the bulbs. Crown Imperial which are temperamental refuse to flower after one year in some parts of the garden, but they are content with an uncomfortable weedy corner of the shaded bed under the trees where in despair I removed them. The tufts of leaves poke up from the leafy soil in February and the orange and mahogany bells appear in early spring.

There is an ancient tradition concerning Crown Imperial lilies in Buckinghamshire, where they are the principal royal flowers in a galaxy of flowers, in the May Day procession at a village near Princes Risborough. Every year for generations the village children of Longwick make garlands of two special shapes, the crown and the sceptre. Cowslips from the hills, bluebells from the woods, tulips and polyanthus from the gardens, all are bound around the withy frames shaped like large open crowns, and tall bulging sceptres. Every crown or sceptre has a Crown Imperial lily, surmounting it, waving its red or gold bells and tufts of green at the top. Inside each floral trophy is a doll, dressed in white with a veil hanging over her. She may represent the Virgin Mary whose day is the First of May, or she may be the pagan spirit of May herself, a memory of an age-old rite of spring in that village which is near the Ichnield Way and the White Cross cut in the chalky surface of the hill.

The crowns are so heavy with their massed flowers, and their curving bands which rise to the summit of the lily, that it takes two children to carry each one, which they sling on two sticks

and bear like a royal trophy. The smallest children carry the wands or sceptres, with a proudly nodding Crown Imperial as tall as the child itself. As they walk in their procession from school to Church, they sing the May Day carol, and the flowers are blessed in Church after a simple service. This is a very old custom, in which the presence of doll, of veil and of

Crown Imperial has some significance which is half lost in the mists of time.

Hidden in the bells of the Crown Imperials are drops, transparent as glass, which are called tears, the "tears of an angel".

The Turk's cap Martagon lily grows anywhere but I have only two or three bulbs of this delicate and fascinating flower. Its purple colour is unusual among the other spring flowers, and the white Martagon is ethereal, a shadow in the shade. This lily is said to be the real hyacinth into which the youth was changed by Apollo. It has the Greek inscription for sorrow — *Ai, Ai* — upon its stem.

Leigh Hunt says, "Now we were struck with the sort of literal black marks with which Turk's Cap is speckled, and we could plainly see that with some allowance quite pardonable in a superstition, the marks might now and then fall together to indicate those characters, *Ai, Ai.*

Now tell your story, Hyacinth, and show
Ai, Ai the more amidst your sanguine woe."

As for the Auratum, which comes from Japan, where it is eaten as a vegetable, this is a golden joy with its scented petals and noble shape. The perfume pervades the air for a great distance. These lilies grow tall and strong, they are lilies of great personality, which I go out to see each day with reverence as if they were archangels alighted in the garden. Like all truly beautiful flowers they make one feel humble to have such infinite wonder on earth.

A parcel of lily bulbs arrived one winter's morning when I was unable through illness to plant them out of doors. In any case the ground was hard as iron under a covering of snow, and I felt in despair as I sorted them into their varieties and thought of the flowers to come. I telephoned for some large plant pots and a bag of John Innes compost, and I planted the lilies; one in each pot, working in the porch. I left the bulbs there for some weeks until I recovered, and to my surprise I saw small dark points appear in the flower pots. Each day a new star of heavy green rose up to the astonished cold world. On fine days I carried them to the garden, but the wind blew the pots over so they were returned to the porch which was slightly sheltered. A blackbird built its nest over them in the spring, and the green shoots grew tall.

At last in May I took some of them into the house, and placed them in a corner of the sitting-room on the floor. Flower-buds appeared and I watered them anxiously. One day a lily unfurled its petals. It was so close to my dining-table I was able to see every detail, as the beak-like bud opened its mouth, the petals uncurled one by one and the stamens pushed themselves apart from the tight bundle in which they lay in the bud. A lily was in full flower, like a burst of music. Then another lily followed, and soon I had seven flowers on one thick stem. It was a Regale lily, of exquisite shape with a personality about it. The room seemed as overjoyed as I was myself. It was a miracle rising from the dark soil. I had never watched flowers so intently as I

watched these lilies unfurl their tight buds, wrapped with such meticulous care by provident nature, packed into so small a compass.

Regale, Tiger Lily, Martagon, Speciosum, and Golden Auratum, they followed one another in five months of beauty. The Auratum was the most spectacular. The buds were each six inches long, and the open flowers were nearly a foot across. They unfolded like umbrellas, with folds sticking together, slowly unlocking and expanding, a petal at a time, curling back with an exquisite fringe on each tip of the petal which turned under. They bent until the curls of the complete flower were displayed, and the brown flecks were revealed. Sweet scents filled the room.

It was a successful experiment, which gave me intense pleasure, and poetry, a favour which I never expected when I planted the bulbs that bitter winter day.

CHAPTER
TEN

Country Words again

Country words still in use come to me from all parts, and lest they should be forgotten with the rapid progress of obliteration which assails our older language, I have collected a few, especially Cornish.

An earthenware jug of large size is called a pitcher, a name which is universally used, but a small pitcher is called a "paddock". It is the size of a jug used at table. A "pig" is a jug.

"Stein" is an earthenware jar with small handles, glazed inside, used for storing lard or for pickling butter. We used these steins.

A 28-lb. jam jar is called a "stug" in Cornwall. We kept these great jars for rhubarb and ginger jam.

A "frail" is a shopping bag or basket, usually made of wicker. It was cheaper than a basket. Frails were used by the very poor as suitcases, fastened with a couple of straps. Japanese baskets were often called "frails".

"Dreve" was used for poor soil.

"Trade" in Cornwall means muddle or rubbish. "I must clean up this trade" — meaning clean up a dirty pond or untidy farmyard.

"Teel" means to plant. "To teel the potatoes" is to plant them. Some speak of teeling the corn.

"Abroad" means open. If a door splits apart it is said to have gone abroad. A box collapsed in the post has gone abroad. "This parcel's gone abroad." "Leave the door abroad" is often used for "Leave the door open".

The crop of a bird is called a "craw". It is Middle English crawe.

"Smeech" is smoke in Cornwall. "I can smell the smeech" says a woman entering a smoky room.

"Fadge" means to get on, to fare well. It occurs in *Love's Labour's Lost*.

"Drexall" is a Cornish word for the ledge at the door bottom.

A "bolly" is a boulder picked up for use in the house, a stone of good shape, probably gathered from the beach to make a doorstop.

Small bits of fat left from rendering lard are called "scratchings" in Derbyshire, "scallops" in Cornwall. In Buckinghamshire they are called "critlings". With them a critling cake is made of flour, critlings, eggs and sugar and it is eaten hot as a great delicacy.

"Hoast" means hoarse in Derbyshire. A man

or beast coughing with a sore throat is said to be hoasting.

"Squinney" means to look askance. "I saw someone squinneying at me." "Dost thou squinney at me?" (*King Lear*, Act IV, Scene 6).

"Planchen" is the upstairs floor (Cornwall), a word much used, from "planch" Middle English, a floor of planks in 1449.

Kittens are still "kitlings" as in the Middle Ages. The Red Lion Inn near my Cheshire home was called The Romping Kitling.

The little blue sheep's bit scabious which grows on the walls is called "headache flower" in Cornwall.

"Nobbly" is a young colt.

"Pitch" is a steep bit of road, a word much used by Buckinghamshire people.

"To swale" is the motion of a candle flame which swings almost horizontal so that wax falls from the candle.

"To dout" is to extinguish and I heard this word recently in my home. "I've douted the fire," cried a maid in dismay.

"A dabbley day" is a wet day, a word Jemima Puddleduck might have used.

"Daunting" is used for regret.

"T" is often used for "d" or "ed". "Take holt of this." "The water is boilt."

"Contrary" and "mischievous" are pronounced with the accent in the middle of the word. This is the old pronunciation and the original one.

"Mouching along" is playing truant, idling like a tramp. A pig mouches and rootles as it hunts under the hedges.

Irises are "flags" and "Lady Luces" are fleur-de-luce.

The moschatel is "Five Faced Bishop".

Wood pigeons are "quiests" and hedge-sparrows are "blue Isaacs".

"Hollin" is often used for holly, "eller" for elder and again this is the old word. "Ellum" is elm.

Oats sown after the cuckoo comes are "cuckoo oats" and they do not flourish.

A quail says "Wet-me-lips" and sometimes the phrase is used for the name of the bird.

The guinea fowl says, "Come back. Come back." My thoughts wing to my home where we had guinea fowl in a corner by the stackyard. I called, "Come back, come back," to them and they answered. They were an enchanting little family.

All little pigs were "chooky-pigs" to us and the smallest a nestle-bird, or runt.

"Lezzur" is a pasture. "Chunter" — to grumble in a soft voice to oneself.

"Snickles" are snares.

"To shrip" is to shred off small pieces, "to lug" is to drag, "to shram" is to be shrivelled up with cold.

"Suent" is smooth, meaning a flowing rhythm.

"Narry" means never, and it is even more emphatic. "Narry a one" is "never a one".

"To tansle" is to beat, or whip.

"Avore" is often used for "before".

"Athirt" is across in Buckinghamshire.

"Chinky" is the Wiltshire chaffinch, in Derbyshire it is "spink". Both these words come from the chirp of the bird.

A "want" is a mole in some counties, whereas in the north we use "moldywarp".

"Puss" is a hare in many counties.

When any game of toys was out of season it was lawful to steal the thing played with. This specially authorized theft was called "smugging". It was expressed by the boys in this doggerel:

> *Tops are in, Spin 'em agin.*
> *Tops are out. Smuggling about.*

and then they seized the top.

Instead of jersey, the navy blue knitted garment which little boys wore was called "ganzey", or guernsey.

Doves were called "dows" or doves with a long "o".

A "bit-bat" was a bat in my childhood.

"Jacky Squealer" is a swift whose high cry pierced the air on summer nights.

Owlets are "ullets" and a newt is an "asker", and the dragon-fly an "edder".

"Long ripple" for snake.

"Appledeane" for a wasp.

"Horniwinks" for peewits.

"Gladdys" for yellow-hammer.

"Crackey" for a wren.

"Mash'n" for a moor-hen — probably abbreviation for marsh-hen.

"Culley" for dipper.

"Peggy dishwasher" for wag-tail.

"Whoa!" or "Whooke!", the cry to stop a horse, is said to be derived from the Latin. It is a translation of the current *"Ohe"*.

A little "frisky" rain in Devonshire is used to mean a drop of rain. As a woman less poetically remarked to me recently, "It's spitting".

"Cow comfort" is the name given to a cattle scratching-post.

"Cuckoo lambs" are late lambs born about the time the cuckoo comes, mid-April. These can be raised on Dartmoor, where it is too cold for early-born lambs.

Children who were ill were "badly".

"A-skirvitting" is dashing about all over the place. A woman in a hurry to go away is "a-skirvitting" round the house.

A "crab's eye" boil, is not quite on the boil.

"The milk's proddling" is the milk is nearly on the boil. This is a universal dialect word for that gentle movement on the surface of boiling milk.

"I remember your faice but I can't call 'ee whome" is a delightful expression for "I cannot remember your name", but it conveys far more in its kindly interest, calling the face home instead of to mind.

"He jewelled it proper, he did" means he treasured it.

"Crossing the drexle" is crossing the threshold in Devon and Cornwall.

A woman always talks of "bagging out" her husband, when she means sending him off with a sandwich lunch.

"Skither the flour" is scatter flour lightly over a pan.

"Tis less snadgerly" means less untidy.

A very slow man is said to be as slow as a snail going to heaven.

"Tallet" is an upper floor or loft (it is a corruption of *tabulatum* — an upper floor).

"Skannelled on to a gibbet" means smashed all to pieces.

"Mors" for roots of trees, still used by Devon people, is Chaucerian English.

"Receipt" was always used by my family and other old country families for recipe. "Can you give me the receipt for rhubarb jam?" we were asked, and there was always a transference of receipts from one family to another. It is the Middle English "receite", but the word is now ousted by recipe. "Recipe" was used in medieval times for medical prescriptions only.

"Middling" meant and still means, "Not very well". It was the sad answer given to enquiries about health.

"Skimmery", is still used for wavering between two decisions.

"Aye" for yes, "Nay" for no are disappearing fast from country talk, but not long ago they were always used.

An author was in the train with some women, travelling through dreary country, and he remarked upon it. "Aye, it's homely," said one of the women. He thought she meant it was her home, whereas she probably used the word in its true meaning of plain but wholesome.

Hardy in *The Mayor of Casterbridge* writes of the attitude to dialect: "One grievous failing of Elizabeth's was her occasional pretty and picturesque use of dialect words — those terrible marks of the beast to the truly genteel.

" 'If you'll bide where you be a minute, father, I'll get it', said the girl. Henchard was angry at her choice of words.

"The sharp reprimand wasn't lost on her," says Hardy, "and in time it came to pass that for 'fay' she said 'succeed', that she no longer spoke of 'dumbledores' but of 'humble bees'; no longer said of young men and women that they 'walked together', but that they were 'engaged'; that she grew to talk of 'greggles' as 'wild hyacinths'; that when she had not slept she did not quaintly tell the servant the next morning that she had been 'hag-rid', but that she had 'suffered from indigestion'."

But these expressions were used with no contumely, no reproach, in every country place, mocked at only by the most barbarous townsman, and certainly Henchard, in Hardy's novel, was no genteel townsman, as he walked the lanes. Hardy was probably mistaken in adding this to his estimate of Henchard's character and cruelty.

CHAPTER
ELEVEN

Casual Encounters

One April day when I was in London I saw an old tramp woman, wearing heavy laced boots, hobbling along like one of the characters out of Dickens. She wore an enormous black felt hat on her grey elf-locks, and a black shawl was draped over a greatcoat, pierced with safety-pins holding the rents together. On her back hung a sack packed full of something. In one hand she carried a thick stick, in the other a large basket like a hamper, packed with clothes, which brimmed out from under the lid. All her worldly goods were with her; she was unique, complete, like a snail with its shell.

She stood looking in a butcher's shop, and I, in a stationary bus, looked too with her eyes. There were strings of sausages, and dishes of juicy chops and joints of meat. She hesitated, and went over the prices in her mind and there she stood, staring and undecided. An elegant young woman came out of the shop, with never a glance at this eternal woman of the earth. She swept past her in her silk coat, unseeing. I longed to spring from the bus, to buy the sausages for her, to hear her voice, and to see the dark gipsy eyes and the wrinkled brown face, but the traffic lights changed and the bus jerked on, and at the same moment the old woman hitched up her bag and slowly went on her way. It was in Davies Street in Mayfair on a day when the cuckoo called from the beech tree before I started in the morning and ice lay on the bird bath, a day of sparkling beauty which had brought out this hibernating old woman to walk in the West End.

I was on my way to see a small exhibition of Dutch pictures. One of the most beautiful, a flower painting by Balthaser Van der Ast had been sold, I was told, the day before. A lady admired it but she could not afford the high price. So she went away but left a parcel behind. She returned shortly afterwards for the parcel, and, looking again at the picture, she asked for a blank cheque. She wrote out the sum of money quickly "before I repent" and then she hurried away. She still left her parcel behind.

How feminine this is and it is the story of the pearl of great price!

Gipsies have gone for many months from the road near my cottage but a short time ago I heard crackling in the woods as men broke down the slender trees for firewood. I saw the scars of smashed branches, and a piece of rag and a tin thrown away. It is the trail of the wanderers. Then in a hollow I came across seven or eight caravans, canary yellow, red and green and blue, assembled in a deserted gravel pit, with washing hanging from the trees and a dozen dogs and some children running about. Four ponies, two piebald and two brown, were grazing in a

narrow croft by the steep lane. It was an encampment of gipsy life which seemed secure and settled with an air of permanence, but the law is for one night only. Gipsies had chosen a secluded spot, for the pit lies under a steep bank hidden from view, warm and sheltered with water, grass and woodland near.

A week later I went again to see them and there were the caravans with their gay colours nestled in the corners of the wood. Perhaps the police had allowed them to stay, and I wondered whether this was to be a permanent home. It was strangely quiet with no children shouting or dogs barking. Then close to my home a young boy burst out of a wood with a heavy stick in his hand with which he had been beating the coppice. He was a bright-eyed lad with dark wavy hair and rosy cheeks and a charm in his manner. I stopped to talk as I held back my angry Scottie.

He told me he came from the camp in the pit and they had been there three days. They were not the people I had seen a week ago.

"We have to move after one night, but we drew in there because my cousin was ill," he explained. "He was took ill at seven o'clock last night and we sent for the doctor at ten o'clock and he died at eleven in the ambulance on the way to hospital."

"How old was your cousin?" I asked.

"He was ten. He wasn't ill before that. He just got ill that day and died. It was bronchitis and pneumonia the doctor said." The little boy spoke sadly. "So they let us stop till he is buried."

He told me his name was Ernie and his sisters were Ruby and Doris. As we talked another boy came out into the lane with half a dozen lurchers and greyhounds, slim quick dogs in good condition and well-trained. The boy was about thirteen but his large jacket slipping from the shoulders and his long grey ragged trousers made him look like a man in the distance. The two boys had been hunting with the dogs while their aunt begged for rags at the houses. They got their living by making clothes pegs, and gaily coloured wooden flowers, chrysanthemums and roses, fashioned from wood shavings and dyed. In winter and summer they work selling the flowers at the markets, walking from village to village.

"We get many a hare, lots of hares," said Ernie. "The dogs catch hares and they used to get rabbits."

I could well believe it, for hares sit bolt upright in the fields, and now and then a pheasant rises with a loud "cuck-cuck", or a pair of partridges scuttle through the thick stubble.

I fumbled in my pocket but I had no money for these jolly boys. They smiled happily and went on and we promised to meet again sometime. Tomorrow is the child's funeral, the little ten-year-old gipsy, dark-eyed and red-cheeked only a week ago.

An old countryman came to see me, hobbling to the backdoor, stiff with rheumatism, his face alight as he thanked me for his Christmas parcel. I gave him Cox's Orange Pippins, tea, cake, mince pies, sweeties, a card and a new half-crown wrapped in a gay paper. He began to talk.

He said he had been sitting with another old man who was infirm and laid up in his bedroom. He goes to sit and talk with him about old times, and they have many a laugh. These two ancients gossip of the time when they paid their garden rent at the Saracen's Head to the Squire — the rent was eighteen pence a year for twenty poles of ground. They sat at the rent audit, each with a pint of beer, a church-warden pipe, new and shining white, and two ounces of tobacco. They sang songs and in the bedroom of the invalid he sang the same songs to remind his friend. There and then in the kitchen he sang to me.

He talked of Holly Bush Common where people made faggots and sold them in High Wycombe, taking them on their backs or in little donkey carts. When he was born, over eighty years ago, his mother had little shirts for him edged with narrow Buckinghamshire lace which she had made. His sons wore the shirts and his grandsons but his granddaughter who had them for the great-grandchildren let them fall to rags.

Nobody liked policemen of the woods, although they were very much nicer than poachers. I used to wander alone in the depths of woodland, wading through thickets of bracken higher than my head, where the light was palest green and the ferny roof over me was like a green-water palace under the sea. I went through brakes of hazel and hawthorn to the little open spaces which I knew very well, where bluebells misted the ground and many a rare flower grew, the tallest foxgloves whose gloves slipped so neatly over my ten fingers as if to disguise me from human eyes, where the sweetest lilies of the valley grew, the pinkest orchids, and always I stepped with exquisite care and shadows of fear, a wild animal myself, lest I should meet the keeper. Wolves and bears perhaps lurked in the woods, but none of them was as fearful as a gamekeeper with a gun under his arm, his leggings tight round his legs, his full-skirted coat with deep pockets which held fur and feather, his bright black eyes and his brown sardonic face. I thought he could shoot me if he liked and bury me under the leaves and nobody would know. So I stepped soft as a feather drifting in the woods, and listened for the crackle of twigs and peered at the ants and beetles and then, when I came round the corner, there he would be, standing like a statue under a tree, waiting to see what kind of animal it was ruffling the bracken tips. Happily we usually saw the keeper before he saw us and we retreated. He was on friendly terms with us, but we did not trust him. The woods were on the sloping hills and from our fields we could see the keeper cross the glades or stand on the crest against the sky.

The uniformed railway man, capless, jacket open, buttons loose, hands in a parcel at the back door, and waits with a cigarette dangling from his lips and I sign the receipt. Then he turns away to his van.

"Bye, bye, Madam," says he.

I am never sure how to reply to this farewell, but I infinitely prefer it to "Ta-ta" which is the good-bye of some others.

The porter at the station is very solicitous over the welfare of the passengers. "Now, my dear," he says, "if ever you want to borrow any money I can help you. If you forget your purse I can lend you up to £5," and I promise to borrow from him when I have been careless.

Kilvert recalls some of the greetings of his day a hundred years ago. "Old Sarah Williams and a few more of the old people still salute one with 'Your servant, sir' and 'Your servant, ma'am'. In the next generation and in a few more years this will never be heard. Some of the old-fashioned folks still call me 'Your Honour' and 'Your Reverence'."

The Irish haymakers of my childhood always used these terms of politeness to my father, but the Irish are proverbially polite. A few days ago I heard of a flustered witness in the box replying to the magistrate and calling him "Your Majesty" to the great delight of everyone. Little American boys domiciled here say "Mam" to a stranger, which is charming. We called our schoolmistress "Mam" in my childhood at the village school, but the two young pupil-teachers were "Miss Poppy" and "Miss Florrie", the Christian names of these long-haired girls, for no one ever used their surnames. In the London bus the con-ductress says "Love" and "Dear". This is a delight to some, but "Ducks" is not so happy.

Long, long ago, I lived for a time near Wimbledon, and the common was my daily pilgrimage to keep a memory of the country in my mind and to help me forget the welter of houses around me. It was my first stay in London. I was told that the poet Swinburne came up the hill from Putney every morning, about twelve o'clock, to go to an inn at the edge of the common. This rather shocked me, for he was my favourite poet, and I was sorry he had to go to an inn to drink, but I determined to see him.

I loitered on Putney Heath, among the gorse bushes and the broken bracken. If he had walked on the common to get inspiration I should have been happier. Then shortly after twelve, he came, a small man with reddish ragged little beard, and piercing blue eyes. I gazed at him with admiration for his poetry, and some surprise that he was an ordinary mortal. His big felt hat hid the long yellow hair, now turning grey. His clothes were shabby and loose and poor. I had expected him to wear a blue cloak and flaming clothes, and I thought his feet would not even touch the ground. He would float along, immortal, always young.

Could old age ever touch a poet? I wondered. Here was the poet who wrote *Atalanta* which I knew by heart.

When the hounds of spring are on winter's traces,
The Mother of months in meadow and plain,
Fills the shadows and windy places
With lisp of leaves and ripple of rain.

I had chanted it in our fields, which were haunted by the old gods, and I had heard the wind bay like the hounds of hell.

He wrote of the swallow, too, our beloved swallow, who nested in the barn where the heavy carts lay.

Swallow, my sister, O sister swallow,
How can thy heart be full of the spring?

There he was, walking without wings on the road, and then he turned into the doorway of a commonplace inn. I was disappointed, and yet I was elated. I had seen Swinburne, the poet of youth and love, the poet of music and the weaver of words. All my poets had been dead men, and here was one alive, drinking, and walking the hard road.

I went away, across the common, thinking deep thoughts of life, puzzled and bewildered at the latter days of genius.

Another casual encounter remains in my memory, with a sharp impact I received at the time, the invasion of my private thoughts. I was going home from London, taking a store of delightful experiences in my mind, to ponder on during the journey. I looked about for an empty carriage at St. Pancras Station and I saw a carriage with only an old lady sitting quietly in a corner. There I could lean back and think of Pavlova in *The Dying Swan*, and go through the music in my heart, I could think of the operas I had seen, and the ballets, all new experiences. I could also savour the welcome home to house and fields. It was a lovely day of spring, and the lambs would be playing. There might even be a cade lamb, white as snow, in the orchard, waiting for me. Would there be young calves to suck my finger? A foal I knew about, for I had heard of it. I would pick primroses that same day and get the country air into my lungs.

So I sat in the comfortable carriage, thinking happily of the country scene, and the people I loved. I was aware as the train gathered speed that the old lady was regarding me intently, but I did not want to talk to anyone. I wrapped my cloak of silence and invisibility around me and I listened to the song of the engine as it ran along the iron road. In utter bliss I watched the houses rush past and the country open out. I was going home, home!

Suddenly the old lady leaned forward and touched my knee. I was startled out of my happiness, I turned to her large moonlike face which bent towards me. What could be the matter with her?

"My dear, I want to ask you something," she said.

"Yes?" I enquired.

"Are you saved?" she said.

I was astounded, and a wave of anger surged over me, but I pushed it away. She was old, she could know nothing of the happiness that filled me to the brim. I must speak patiently to her. She repeated her question.

"Tell me, are you saved?"

"I hope so. Yes, I am sure I am," I replied, smiling. "I have never been otherwise."

She seemed disappointed, she thought I did not understand, but I had heard the question before in extreme youth. It was asked at Revival meetings when I went with the servant girl and we all knelt on the grass in the large tent pitched in a field like a circus tent. We sang hymns, which I liked, and then the famous revivalist and his helpers worked us up to a passion of confession and weeping and alleluias, as people went up to the Mercy Seat. This always alarmed me, I thought they were murderers and drunkards, and I, a little girl, knelt close to the sheltering arm of the warm-hearted maid. Now I was being drawn to the Mercy Seat in an express train with no escape.

"Do you love God?" asked the lady, sternly.

"Yes," I answered, surprised, for ours was no era of doubts.

"Are you sure? Are you happy?" she asked, probing to find a chink in my armour.

"Yes, I am the happiest person in the world," said I, boldly, and indeed I thought I was.

She hesitated a moment and then she went on.

"Let us kneel down in prayer," said she.

I looked at the dusty carriage floor, and my light dress, but I had often knelt on the hard stone kitchen floor for family prayers. She spread her handkerchief for herself, and we both knelt in some discomfort between the narrow seats. My ignoble fear was that the train might stop and somebody might come in and find us down there in the dust, and how could we explain?

She said the Lord's Prayer and I said it too. I think she was surprised that I knew it. Then she said a short prayer, commending me to God and asking Him to take care of me, and to give me light. I felt vulnerable as I knelt there, with the carriage rocking with speed and the country streaming past, as if we were really rushing up to heaven's gates. I was touched by the old lady's solicitude, but I was indignant that she had entered my own privacy. Why did she think I was a lost soul?

We rose from our knees, dusted ourselves and sat back in our corners. We were silent. I could not return to my dreams, I was glad when we arrived at our county town and I could alight and change to the slow old puffing train packed with country people returning from the local market. We smiled and we parted, a casual encounter that surprised and embarrassed me with the direct questions about my inner life. How did anyone know whether they were saved or not? What did it mean? I knew what it meant, but the words were wrong. A sense of the divine in all things I had, with the earth as clear as glass, and I felt that I knew the secret heart of life and death. Paradise was near, and the invisible was revealed all around me, but "saved" implied an escape from shipwreck, and I might prefer to go down with the ship.

CHAPTER
TWELVE

Some Thoughts on Cellars

It is well known that the rambling old houses of childhood held far more terrors for the young that the neat little model dwellings where there is no room for a boggart and even a thin ghost might find it difficult to conceal itself; but the instinctive fears of childhood, the inherent instincts of what-you-will persist throughout all the explanations of the psychologist. The bear under the bed, the lion in the passage, the creature hiding in the shadows, they still exist, in spite of commonsense denials, and the phantoms of dream are perhaps stronger with the food they receive from films and television.

The great exorciser of these childhood fears is light — and not candlelight or moonlight but the sudden blaze from the electric lamp at the magical touch of the switch. Gaslight has not this power of scaring away the evil ones, for there is the interval between the scratch of the match and the flare of the yellow flame after the tap is turned, and this interval can be of the duration of eternity. Matches, too, have a power of disappearing at the moment of crisis, and one remembers the story of the man in a haunted room who in the darkness stretched out his hand to seek the matches, only to receive a box which was placed in his fingers by the ice-cold paw of a ghostly visitant. Electricity brings comfort of sudden light illuminating every corner and (for

the first time in life) the demons of darkness are exorcized. They flee into dark cupboards, they flatten themselves among the clothes in the wardrobe, a place they have often haunted. They flee down to the cellars.

These underground caves were unknown in my country life. The houses had the living rock for foundations upon which the stone structure was built. In the small Cheshire house where I lived when I was first married I saw my first cellar. The house was seventeenth century and this cellar was admired by everyone who saw it as a romantic place. We reached it by a carved oak staircase with fine balusters which had square newels at the corners, and broad shallow steps which led down from the hall. A little green door with glass panels led off the cellar stairs to the garden, half-way down, and then we continued, holding the smooth seventeenth-century oak handrail to the bottom, where we walked on stone floors and entered the rooms. They had been used as a garden room, a wash house and a wine cellar. They were fresh and clean and bright in the sunshine, whitewashed and painted green, and lighted by windows. Who would have guessed how sinister the cellars would look in a cataract of moonlight? What kind of face might appear pressed against the window glass of the door to the garden? A "face of crumpled linen" might easily look in. Who might lurk in those underground rooms, what spectre from the house's ancient past when the Cranford ladies had knocked on that very door? Who might step lightly up the flight of stairs, appearing round the corner where the staircase turned at right angles? What ghost from another century would walk there? I was alarmed and I was silent, but the house was not silent. Little feet of mice scampered about down there and rustles and groans came from the timbers. The house was lighted by gas but the cellars and passages had nothing to illuminate them, so I carried a candle and the long shadows dipped and curtsied and shot up to the ceiling and fell to the stairway as my hand shook. Every night there was an ordeal to go upstairs and to come down from my bedroom, to pass the corner of the broad stairway which led downwards to, the cellars, where who-knows-what were having jinks down below. In a flash something might scuttle up the stairs and seize me. I was often alone till late at night and I sat in the panelled little parlour reading or playing the piano, unwilling to pass that open stairway.

Yet nothing came up the stairs, no ghost appeared, only whispers and sighs and gentle murmurs which made my hair stand on end and my cheeks turn scarlet as I took up my candle and went up the stairs, determined to put my fears to flight.

Another home in Cheshire had several cellars, for this bottom floor was an integral part of the house, it could not be avoided, for one room was the coal-cellar, another with curved roof the wine cellar where cider was kept, a third was the larder, and the fourth the wash-kitchen, with fireplace and copper for boiling clothes and hanging lines complete. There were windows to the garden and all was light with an apple tree outside on the small green lawn. No ghosts lived in this early Victorian house. There was electric light, too, and the steep stair was a plain wooden staircase with a narrow handrail and no lovely open balusters and newels of oak. It was closed at the top by a door which could be locked and bolted to keep the ghosts safe.

The larder was icy cold. It was a lofty room, whitewashed and dim with a great stone table in the centre upon which stood the meat-safe. Above it suspended from the ceiling by four wooden posts was a square shelf the same size as the stone table. Great hooks were fixed to the ceiling for hanging game.

The floor was made of old uneven bricks, which were swilled once a week, and the water drained away through a grid. There was room enough for mighty joints and scores of pies on the shelves which ran round the walls. The butter was frozen down in those depths and the food kept fresher than in any place I know, with the open window and the cool depths of the earth.

There was none of the trepidation and sense of ghostly inhabitants in that series of cellars, with the lights and the closeness to the house above, and I never minded running down the staircase to these spacious underground rooms. The wash-cellar was a gay, happy place, with its blazing fire under the copper every Monday morning, and its clothes baskets and little rubber mangle and dolly-tub, and its glimpses of blackbirds on the lawn and roses on the old white rosebush. On wet days we could light the fire in the early Victorian fireplace with its elaborate open grate and dry the clothes on the lines in the cellar. We could chop sticks and paint and fashion simple toys down there.

In spite of my affection for this cellar, with its curls of steam and its smell of fire and oil and sticks, for it was also the wood store and the paint shop and the carpenter's room, there was a queer nagging little fear connected with it which came out to me at night. It was the Victorian melodrama room such as one saw later in *Arsenic and Old Lace* and *The Week-end Cottage*. In fancy it was the kind of place where bodies might be buried, down under those irregular bricks. In the daylight this was forgotten, we ran singing down the cellar stairs, my little maid and I, for meat or vegetables, for cider and gooseberry pies, but at night the door was shut and bolted and the cellar was not entered unless there were people in the house to come to the rescue of the adventurer. Yes, cellars were useful but they made extra work with the flight of stairs and they were the haunts of the unknown who might be lurking down there. They have gone out of fashion, they are forgotten.

But they are missed, these deep haunts of the invisible, for they were wonderful storehouses, like caves in the earth. They were refrigerators without electricity to work them, they kept the food cool and good in hot weather, they were the extra capacity of the house which made it self-contained with no extra area, with coal and wood, with workshop and drying room, all under one roof. They kept the house dry, by the circulation of air under it, and they could be used to keep a burglar waiting for the police, a lock-up.

LARGE PRINT

If you have enjoyed reading this book, you will be pleased to know that many more titles are available.

We have listed a selection on the next few pages. These are printed in large print and some are also published by Isis in unabridged audio form. In addition, there are other titles, not listed here, which are only available from us as audio books.

Further information on these and many other titles, is available from the address below. Alternatively, contact your local library for details of what they have.

Any suggestions you may have for new large print or audio titles, would be very welcome.

ISIS
55 St Thomas' Street
Oxford OX1 1JG
(0865) 250333

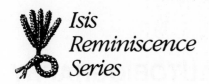

*Isis
Reminiscence
Series*

Available in either hardback or softback, these titles are chosen for their memory-evoking content.

Fred Archer	**Poachers Pie**
Ida Gandy	**A Wiltshire Childhood**
Bill Naughton	**On the Pig's Back, An Autobiographical Excursion**
Walter Rose	**The Village Carpenter**
Flora Thompson	**Heatherley**
Alison Uttley	**Country Things**

BIOGRAPHY AND AUTOBIOGRAPHY

Lord Abercromby	**Childhood Memories**
Margery Allingham	**The Oaken Heart**
Hilary Bailey	**Vera Brittain**
Trevor Barnes	**Terry Waite**
Winifred Beechey	**The Rich Mrs Robinson**
Sidney Biddle Barrows	**Mayflower Madam**
Christabel Bielenberg	**The Past Is Myself**
Ian Botham	**It Sort of Clicks**
Michael Burn	**Mary and Richard**
Winston S Churchill	**Memories and Adventures**
Denis Constanduros	**My Grandfather**
George Courtauld	**Odd Noises From the Barn**
Mary Craig	**The Crystal Spirit**
Peter Evans	**Ari**
Diana Farr	**Five at 10**
Joyce Fussey	**Calf Love**

BIOGRAPHY AND AUTOBIOGRAPHY

Joyce Fussey	**Cats in the Coffee**
Joyce Fussey	**Cows in the Corn**
Jon & Rumer Godden	**Two Under the Indian Sun**
William Golding	**The Hot Gates**
Michael Green	**The Boy Who Shot Down an Airship**
Michael Green	**Nobody Hurt in Small Earthquake**
Unity Hall	**Philip**
Unity Hall & Ingrid Seward	**Royalty Revealed**
Penny Junor	**Charles**
Imran Khan	**All Round View**
Julia Keay	**The Spy Who Never Was**
Margaret Lane	**The Tale of Beatrix Potter**
T E Lawrence	**Revolt in the Desert**
Bernard Levin	**The Way We Live Now**
Suzanne Lowry	**Cult of Diana**
Vincent V Loomis with Jeffrey L Ethell	**Amelia Earhart**

BIOGRAPHY AND AUTOBIOGRAPHY

Eugene McCarthy	**Up 'Til Now**
Jeanine McMullen	**Wind in the Ash Tree**
Peter Medawar	**Memoir of a Thinking Radish**
Spike Milligan	**Adolf Hitler: My Part in his Downfall** (A)
Jessica Mitford	**Hons and Rebels**
Eric Newby	**Something Wholesale**
Christopher Nolan	**Under the Eye of the Clock** (A)
Gerald Priestland	**The Unquiet Suitcase**
Siegfried Sassoon	**Memoirs of an Infantry Officer**
Ingrid Seward	**Diana**
Dolly Shepherd	**When the 'Chute Went Up**
Isaac Bashevis Singer	**Love and Exile**
Norman Tebbit	**Upwardly Mobile**
Andrew Thomson	**Margaret Thatcher**
Robert Westall	**The Children of the Blitz**
Ben Wicks	**The Day They Took The Children**

General Non-Fiction

Michael Bright	**The Living World**
Estelle Catlett	**Track Down Your Ancestors**
Bruce Chatwin	**What Am I Doing Here**
Phil Drabble	**One Man and His Dog**
Jonathan Goodman	**The Lady Killers**
Anita Guyton	**Healthy Houseplants A-Z**
Duff Hart-Davis	**Country Matters**
William R Hartson	**Teach Yourself Chess**
Stephen W Hawking	**A Brief History of Time**
Dr Richard Lacey	**Safe Shopping, Safe Cooking, Safe Eating**
Doris Lessing	**Particularly Cats and More Cats**
Vera Lynn	**We'll Meet Again**
Desmond Morris	**The Animals Roadshow**
Desmond Morris	**Dogwatching**
Desmond Morris	**Catlore**
Frank Muir & Denis Norden	**You Have My Word**
Shiva Naipaul	**An Unfinished Journey**
John Pilger	**A Secret Country**
R W F Poole	**A Backwoodsman's Year**
Valerie Porter	**Faithful Companions**
Beryl Reid	**Beryl, Food and Friends**
Sonia Roberts	**The Right Way to Keep Pet Birds**
Yvonne Roberts	**Animal Heroes**
June Whitfield	**Dogs' Tales**
Ian Wilson	**Undiscovered**
Andrew Young	**A Prospect of Flowers**

History, War and Reminiscences

Charles Allen	**Plain Tales from the Raj**
William Bligh	**An Account of the**
Robert Bowman (ed.)	**Mutiny on HMS Bounty**
John P Eaton &	
Charles Hass	**Titanic: Destination Disaster**
Richard Garrett	**Great Escapes of World War II**
John Harris	**Dunkirk**
Angela Lambert	**1939: The Last Season of Peace**
Frank Pearce	**Sea War**

Poetry and Drama

Lord Birkenhead	**John Betjeman's Early Poems**
Joan Duce	**I Remember, I Remember...**
Joan Duce	**Remember, If You Will...**
Dan Sutherland	**Six Miniatures**
Herbert W Wood	**And All Shall Be Well**

Cookery

Rabbi Lionel Blue	**Kitchen Blues**
Rose Elliot	**Your Very Good Health**
Grace Mulligan	**Farmhouse Kitchen**
Jennifer Davies	**The Victorian Kitchen**

Reference and Dictionaries

Moyra Bremner	**Supertips to Make Life Easy**
Margaret Ford	**In Touch at Home**
	The Lion Concise Bible Encyclopedia
	The Longman English Dictionary
	The Longman Medical Dictionary
	Longman Thesaurus

Short Stories

Angela Carter	**Fireworks**
Colette	**Gigi** and **The Cat**
A E Coppard	**The Higgler and Other Stories**
Roald Dahl	**Kiss Kiss**
Leon Garfield	**Shakespeare Stories**
Thomas Hardy	**Wessex Tales**
Nathaniel Hawthorne	**Tanglewood Tales**
Henry James	**Daisy Miller and other stories**
M R James	**A Warning to the Curious** (A)
D H Lawrence	**Love Among the Haystacks** (A)
Saki	**Beasts and Super-beasts**
Alan Sillitoe	**The Far Side of the Street**
Peter Ustinov	**The Disinformer**
Robert Westall	**Antique Dust**
Marguerite Yourcenar	**Oriental Tales**

(A) Large Print books available in Audio

Humour

Douglas Adams	**The Hitch Hiker's Guide to the Galaxy**
Mary Dunn	**Lady Addle Remembers**
	Echoes of Laughter
Giovanni Guareschi	**Don Camillo and the Devil**
Barry Pain	**The Eliza Stories**
Walter Carruthers Sellar &
Robert Julian Yeatman	**1066 And All That**
Tom Sharpe	**Blott on the Landscape**
Tom Sharpe	**Porterhouse Blue**
Tom Sharpe	**Vintage Stuff** (A)
Tom Sharpe	**Wilt on High**
E OE Somerville &
Martin Ross	**In Mr Knox's Country**
Sue Townsend	**True Confessions of Adrian Albert Mole, Margaret Hilda Roberts and Susan Lilian Townsend**

(A) Large Print books available in Audio